ECO-NOMICS

A SUSTAINABILITY REVOLUTION

ROMAN SENONER

CONTENTS

Introduction   v

PART I
UNSUSTAINABLE ECONOMICS

1. The Ideal Society   3
2. Trapped in old ideas   20
3. The Myth of the economic hero   37
4. An exploitation Doctrine   54
5. Monetizing of nature   68

PART II
ECONOMICS FOR THE FUTURE

6. The affordability paradox   83
7. Reclaiming the state   96
8. Shaping a prosperous and sustainable society   107
9. Putting it together   121

About the Author   131

INTRODUCTION

In a time such as this, when you hear politicians on TV telling the world that we need "more growth" and "more productivity" whilst, at the same time, experts warn us that we need to scale back the human impact on nature massively, you may wonder - what is going on here?! Don't they talk to each other? Do they live in parallel universes?

Can we combine getting to know the basics in economics, while also determining the economic falsehoods that we are suffering from and, at the same time, laying out a plan for hardwiring sustainability into the financial system? I know this sounds like three books in one, but I will try to cover all three topics in straightforward language and articulate the issues that need to be understood and addressed if a change is to occur. This book is intended for readers of any level. No jargon is present in this book, to make it accessible to all and to spread understanding of the basic notions of how economics and environmental damage are interrelated and how unsustainable our current economic model truly is. In this book, we will examine the causes, relationships, and solutions that are in our hands and that we must use if we are serious about moving towards a sustainable society.

Society does not only include the economy. We should take a broader approach to become the much-needed sustainable society that is necessary to overcome both current and future crises. We will need to explore other fields that can bring the community forward, namely those of justice and equality, which are a necessity to true sustainability, as I will argue in the book. It took me months to develop this book, and I have grown increasingly more worried while writing it, about whether or not we can master the immense challenges that await us. Surprisingly, though, I have become more optimistic too, as I realized the enormity of the possibilities we have at our feet. So, this book is solution-oriented and a declaration of hope for the future.

In writing this book, I have relied heavily on many sources, with the economics part mainly based on the insights of modern money theory (MMT), which is, at its core, how the contemporary paper money system works. From this, we can gain incredible insight and understanding of the extreme flexibility it offers, as well as the potential it holds to put society in an almost perfect state of efficiency, productivity, and efficacy.

These insights from MMT, as well as those from the heterodox (not mainstream theory) that are currently gaining substantial attention from the mainstream, will be instrumental in utilizing our full potential as a society to master both present and future challenges. As these theories gain more and more adherents, their incredible possibilities for transforming our economic and monetary systems will be realized. This book is to give you an idea of what can be achieved and lay out a non-utopian plan to hardwire sustainability in our societal organization - which should be the aim of any concerned citizen, seeing the environmental catastrophes unfolding before their eyes.

This book will base its insights on MMT (modern monetary theory) but will also try to move beyond this brand of discipline, as it is still focused on what I call "wealth creation," which is the monetizing of natural ecosystems to build private wealth. We need to move away from this and towards a paradigm focused on wealth allocation: one that creates prosperity but is also sustainable. The economics that takes into consideration the future while still exploiting the utility of the capitalist free market and the competition, innovation, and efficiency it delivers is the way forward.

Currently, we see a considerable rise in the popularity of these topics of the waning environments, particularly by young people that fear their future. They start to protest things on a political level and point out the absurdities of going forward with a system that is self-destructing. While their proposals are laudable and they succeeded in raising and furthering the awareness of our unsustainable way of life, without an economic plan, it is impossible to have accomplish these political intentions regarding the sustainability of our economy. It is economics that lays the base for how our economy works. Without revolutionizing this social science, we will not succeed. No matter how good our intent is or how much we will work on it, it is a fight against windmills if we don't put things right on the theory level that economics handles.

Economics is too important of a topic to leave in the hands of those unelected high priests - the economists who goad the rulers of the world with their mystic auras and predictions. This science is really what gives them the power to be such masters and have such control of the entire economic system. This book will bring the basics to the awareness of the reader while pointing out how and why the current system is so damaging. It will also point out that the theory is the problem and that a new economic thinking will offer us a new perspective regarding our quest for sustainability and what we could reach if we were to use the full potential of the industrial machine we have in our hands.

Through this book, I will provide a way to solve the current environmental calamities that are piling up and that need urgent action. In that way, I will give the right answer that can only come from the economics perspective and point of view. An extremely urgent answer will be provided to these emergencies and will be a starting point to what I hope is an extremely logical and pragmatic approach towards sustainability.

I

UNSUSTAINABLE ECONOMICS

1

THE IDEAL SOCIETY

AVE you ever wondered why the "progress" that we often speak about in our societies does not seem to get to us as individual entities, why we often seem to go backward in terms of personal wellbeing? When it comes to technology, we have made considerable progress with our capabilities and achieving our potential. When it comes to new developments in society, the tremendous speed of today's world is a perfect example. If the current rate of change continues, every aspect of our culture will soon be completely automatized.

Robots could soon account for the majority of our workforce, replacing tedious manual labor. Full automation will become a reality in the not too distant future, with new technological advancements emerging each year. Our actual wellbeing and the impact this will have on the lives of individuals are more complicated, though. Our potential for developing machines to enhance productivity and automation has not lived up to its expectations in regards to personal wellbeing. Did it translate into a better outcome and lives for a majority? If you look at the current state of society, the answer is a definite "No!"

The hard realities of today's society paint a radically different image of things, with most people living in neighborhoods not looking like what we may have optimistically pictured they might just a few short decades ago. Most people's day to day lives often resemble the polar opposite, more of a nightmare than a dream. What we see more and more commonly is financial deprivation; many people struggle to get their families a decent way of living, and most people are exposed to the current rat race that forces them to work more hours for the same wage.

We are currently living in a society of scarcity, even though our productivity levels have never been as abundant. The reason for this situation should be of interest to all, as we are currently like a bunch of lemmings doing things we shouldn't do, slowly bringing us closer to the cliff's edge. We are running around, running out of time, with each decade passing, earning less money from wages when compared to the cost of living.

Why has our incredible knowledge, technology, and skills not benefited us as we thought they would? Why have the things intended to make life easier not done so?

Thousands of years ago, humans had the lifestyle of gatherer/hunters. It is believed that life was characterized by hardship at that time. People had to move around to survive, to follow the natural conditions that were more conducive to growth. Many studies claim this lifestyle was pretty healthy, as nature provided them with everything they needed to live. There were groups of people that freely helped each other. An example of this healthier life can be seen in the bones of clan members that had been medicated. We can presume then that they had a lot of free time, enough for their favorite activities and family, leading to healthier lifestyles for their bodies, compared with the way we lived for the past few hundred years — for example, people working in mines and dying at a young age of pneumonia.

If you trust those studies and look at what they tell us about our quality of life, you may conclude that we have regressed over time. With more and more capabilities, our working hours have increased in the last 50 years. The rat-race of today is claiming many casualties from various burnout syndromes and other stress-related illnesses.

With all the progress, all the agricultural capabilities, all the skills and knowledge, all the power over the natural world, why are people still working themselves into sickness and struggling massively, living in scarcity?

I will give you a hint: we're doing things wrong at an organizational level. We are organizing and allocating resources and labor in an inefficient way.

It is an urgent question to answer. The direction in which we are headed is the wrong one. We can do better than this based on all the capabilities and experience we possess in this modern-day world.

Economics as the Top Organizer of Society

The social science used to organize and allocate the resources of a society is called **economics**. It is the science used to explain and develop theories to organize a community and its resources in the best way possible. It also addresses the needs of the individual and the general interest of the population to reach the optimal result and optimal satisfaction for all involved.

Economics then, in a practical sense, is regarded as the optimal organization, allocation, and management of available resources to achieve the most efficient distribution of goods and services, improve behavior, and facilitate smooth interactions of economic agents. From an energy efficiency point of view, the analogy of economics could be one of seeking the shortest route of energy flowing from one place to the next, with the least resistance.

Economics can be understood easily by leaving out all the noise and incorrect assumptions. Once liberated from this fog, we can start to draw up a plan for reaching more positive outcomes. We need a clear understanding of our possibilities under the current economic system to master the challenges ahead of us. The science of economics undoubtedly overlaps into politics, and I would even argue it overlaps into sociology and philosophy, as it encompasses the behavior of people. In short, economics is based on ideas. Ideas are what shape and enable different theories; therefore, their resulting outcomes are inherently interconnected.

The different economic theories, with its imprinted ideas, will have radically different real-world results. Therefore, ideology, too, will play an integral part in the end-results that will appear in economic study. The various schools of thought in the field of economics that create the current system try to describe it and thus influence it, as well as consequently base their "prescriptions" on it. Our economic systems have been "**built**" through time as they went through testing, trial, and error, mostly by businessmen, bankers, and traders alongside economists, from the start of the 17th century as this social science came into existence. This system occurred by describing and trying to extrapolate the theories that regulate supply and demand, as well as by applying their ideas to render the system more favorable to their own desired outcomes.

As the distribution and allocation of resources and who should benefit are the main contributors to the current problems that we have in our day and age, it is economics that should be the primary tool used to resolve this issue. I say that because economics is a science that has regressed in recent years, instead of progressing to achieve better outcomes. So, for a better organization of society and to achieve the required upheaval, a sound understanding of the basics of economics is imperative if we are to have the necessary tools to create the world we desire.

The ideal way to achieve this is by having the masses understand the importance of "basic economics." It is the only way change can be possible, so people don't fall for the myths that are still propagated today by the media, politicians, and even by many economists. Economics needs to be understood by the regular people to make economists (and politicians) more accountable for their choices. Only an educated population will bring the much-needed change.

Ideas shape outcomes

The mainstream *orthodoxy*, what the current consensus of ideas is called, states that we have to deal with scarce resources and accept this as an unchanging reality. This is a claim that we can't merely accept because it will significantly influence the fundamentals on which a theory bases its validity. It is only a fallacy since it is clear that we live in a world of incredibly abundant resources.

But, even more fundamentally visible to economics is that, generally speaking, demand will promote supply. The question can be raised here that some goods can only be produced in limited quantities, but take for example the car industry - it was undoubtedly the case that the first manufacturers in the early 20th century had low outputs and that their cars were a luxury commodity only for wealthy individuals. This is not the case today, though. We have an overproduction of vehicles since there are not enough buyers. This is due to their production being done more efficiently over time. So then, it is true that the commodity that we intend to produce or the resource that we want to exploit will become more readily available as its successive production stages greatly expand production - until it is rendered a common commodity that is easily accessible to all.

Then there is the case that actual financial wealth should be somewhat scarce, as it is the only way to ensure the demand for it, but that doesn't mean we have a scarcity of natural or human resources; the contrary is often the case. Thus, the mentality of scarcity, whether that of human or natural resources, is not accurate, and this shortsighted "organizational" approach, the premise of many economic textbooks, is simply wrong. An economic doctrine, with its prescriptions based on such vague and fallacious logic of intrinsic scarcity of resources, will project these ideas on the economy it intends to cure. And that is precisely the case, as you will see throughout this book. Applying a sense of scarcity to the economy is an outdated relic from the thinking of past eras.

This is a central topic that we will analyze throughout the book; as such, a claim that we have to deal with scarcity as a guiding principle of science that is based on ideas will undoubtedly have profound repercussions on the policies that are created. There is no doubt then that this is the field we sorely lack in understanding as a society. We don't give it enough consideration when it comes to the operational aspects of organizations, and we fail to harness its potential to progress in any way to bring about real development of our living conditions.

One reason we haven't progressed on this operational layer of society is that political struggles have often overshadowed the battle of ideas. The main problem here is that ordinary people overlook economics, usually being deemed merely too challenging and involved a science to grasp. This is because social science is not a purely empirical field of study but one based on ideas that massively influence outcomes, so it is not easy to understand.

These diverse schools of thought often run counter-arguments to one another, and the same counter-prescriptive natures of which can also be found throughout economics. This is the reason it has been left in the hands of "experts," both by the regular people as well by our politicians. We have commissioned this task to be resolved for us and shirked all responsibility for the aspects of organizing a society in the best way possible.

Politicians rely on faith when it comes to economics and trust that these **"high priests"** will make the "right" decisions then trust us to take their prescriptions at face value. It is easy to understand why, because it can be so confusing. The jargon used by "experts" makes even the most insightful people shy away from understanding it. As a result, voters too mostly rely on faith in these experts' ideas to guide their decision making, since they can't seem to gain a working understanding of this confusing topic for themselves.

Without an understanding of some level of sound economics, no political movement can ever hope to reach their goals, since the way you organize who benefits economically in society will have a massive influence on the result. A big reason for the current political maladies that we suffer from is that voters are easily manipulated and scared into positions that don't benefit them and their economic place in society.

The implications of not understanding how economics functions, or the lack thereof, makes it almost impossible for political movements that promote changing the old, destructive ways to implement any substantial changes. To put it this way - if you don't understand the nature of the suboptimal systems, you will have a hard time changing them. What is essential, then, is to have at least a basic understanding of the economic mechanics at work - to understand how the money system and the laws of supply and demand function. In this book, I will put forward the case that understanding at least some of the primary economic principles, and how they shape societal outcomes, will remove the myopia currently hindering us as a society. Without doing this, we can't reach our full potential or understand what political possibilities we have within our reach.

The misunderstanding in modern economics is caused by the misrepresentation of causes and symptoms. It is a model that doesn't recognize or chooses to ignore that we have a vast abundance of resources at our disposal. This archaic system of thought is dependent upon not finding a way of distributing this abundance of funds for the common benefit of all people. This incredible shortsighted "organizational" approach is the cause of our current demise, and there is an undeniable need for the right kind of economic thinking to take its place, to determine more rational objectives, and to deliver truly effective "cures."

Fortunately, with the right insight, it is relatively straightforward to discredit these fallacious ideas that afflict us when it comes to economic theory. These ideas are roadblocks to our advancing as a society in a positive manner and thus heavily narrow our potential for change.

Once one understands these ideas, one can look at the system from the "outside" without being confused and mistaking symptoms within the system as causes. It also gives us a clear view of what we can accomplish and improve, how we can build our economy and society as we please, and arrive at a more harmonious societal structure.

It is the purpose of this book to clear the fog. I hope to convey the idea that everyone, if interested, can understand these basic concepts of economics. The economic system that has emerged in our society and its practices can be easily explained and understood. That is if one examines only the facts and evidence. The overall functioning, without these unnecessary details and ideologies, is relatively straightforward!

We will cover these basic principles in the first part of this book by looking at what is truly holding us back. This often comes in the form of "ideological" limits imposed by mainstream economics that prevent us from reaching our true potential.

The Elephant in the Room

One of the most significant failures in the subject of economics has been the exclusion of the variable of time. We created systems that didn't include sustainability, and this has been ignored. This renders the current model harmful. Our current organizational systems are not only having detrimental effects on our "financial prosperity" but are endangering the natural ecosystems that sustain our life on earth. A concept that we must incorporate and implement in our economic structures within the next 20 years is the concept of real wealth in the sense of sustainability. We must make the current system compatible with the natural world and not have it operate at its expense.

Nature has developed its ecosystems precisely, with future sustainability arguably being a guiding principle. Anything that comes from the natural world is biodegradable, while the vast majority of things we have built and sold in the past 100 years is not. How can we not include the future "cost" of non-biodegradable materials, such as plastic, in our economics? It will take centuries to degrade fully, and even then, it will only degrade into smaller particles. This is something that will cause damage to humans, animals, and plants for centuries to come... We wholly ignored sustainability during the development of the current system. The fact is, current methods of production were a bad idea in the beginning, mostly because of the unforeseen environmental cost to be paid in the future. The plastic disaster is a perfect example of such foolish thinking.

Not only that, but we are thinking in ways that are based upon the destruction of nature to create "wealth." We equate wealth in today's society with what is regarded as financial wealth, while we don't recognize that other types of wealth are equally important or perhaps even more critical. If we destroy the hospitable environment of our planet, then what worth can financial wealth possibly have? A Native-American saying comes to mind here:

"Once you have caught all the fish, cut all the wood, and poisoned all the waters, you will realize that you can't eat or drink money."

In a world where the balance of nature has been contaminated, resulting in a grey, lifeless, colorless world, the question is - what worth could a million dollars possibly have in such a place? Yet we still chase the paradigm of infinite growth, even though the world, by definition, is finite with limits and boundaries. We are trapped in a mindset of "wealth creation." We have to move towards a more responsible one of wealth administration. That's where economics has to step in and take steps towards rendering our way of life more compatible with the planet.

I will propose a change in name here or, better yet, an addition of a single hyphen to the word "economics," to *eco-nomics*, in the hopes that it will become a harmonious integration of ecosystems with our economic systems. Then, the current ideas fail on all fronts, so we will have to find different ones that work to reach a sustainable society. We have to see the big picture. It is challenging, to say the least, as we come from 300 years of enormous overproduction, overexploitation, and the sacrificing of vital ecosystems that would otherwise guarantee our survival. Sadly, many of these have been heavily compromised.

We have destroyed, over the centuries, a finely tuned environmental system, one that had previously adapted to agricultural production as a way of sustaining ourselves. Over the last 300 years, though, our rate of production has skyrocketed, and we have pillaged many parts of the natural world, establishing ourselves as a virus of consumption. These actions have, and continue to cause, repercussions that irreversibly tarnish our livable environment. We should abandon this reckless pursuit of growth today, as this economic model has no future; it can't go on like this. Now, of course, we can't do this because we have to sustain our families. We are stuck in a cul-de-sac with the only way out being new economic frameworks, and it is the purpose of this book to lay out such concepts.

The good news is that we don't have to give up "wealth" to reach a better outcome, and that may seem counterintuitive at first. There is proof that we can have both; we can preserve nature while maintaining the benefits we have in our modern societies. This is a very high claim, but in this book, I will prove it is achievable. So let me make something abundantly clear now; a prosperous society and a more utopian social structure *are entirely achievable.*

As I will explain in the following chapters, the hard part is not the creation of financial "**wealth**" but rather the addressing of a rapidly approaching bottleneck - the environmental crisis.

Shaping the outcomes that we want

The good news is that we don't need a drastic overhaul of the entire system. Instead, we need to tweak mechanisms within the system to put us on the right course, though it needs to be done relatively quickly. We will cover this in more detail in the first part of this book by looking at what is truly holding us back. The reality is that we don't lack the funds to have our ideal society, but there are ideological reasons, rather than hardwired limits, that prevent us from reaching such an optimal state of societal organization.

The approach to preach and moralize to people to bring the necessary change will not work either. Instead, with economics, we have the keys to change our societal structure on a far more fundamental level. We must hardwire the public consciousness into desiring to shape the environmental conditions that we want, to have a more stable and sustainable economy. In this sense, we are the gods of our destiny; the key is in understanding and shaping our guiding principles to have the world that we want. It is a lost science, as politics and voters alike have wholly given up the "hardwiring" part to these unaccountable high priests.

Economics has decoupled from the struggles of the majority of the regular folks and has become too much theory found in books... It has left the field of evidence. And here lies the basic understanding that these high priests lack. Rather than obsessing about accounting, governmental finances, and national debt, we have to rebuild economics based on the visions and the first-hand experiences of those it impacts. In other words, we have to embody the outcomes that we wish to see in the economy.

In economics, this approach is called functional finance and was used to significant effect in the postwar years, though it has fallen out of favor since. For example, we have followed *"full employment policies"* in the past through massive government spending on construction after WW2 to improve public infrastructure, creating a vast number of jobs for the unemployed in the process (such as the construction of the Hoover Dam, as well many of America's bridges and road networks). This was a time when we indeed had almost 100% employment, and we reaped tremendous societal benefits as a result, without resorting simply to handing out money to the unemployed. Ideas shape outcomes, and we have since strayed from this path, with the common mantra of our times being that *"we can't afford it!"*

But back then, not only could we "afford it," but actually, we created the conditions we wanted in the economy; we were in the driver's seat of the economic car. It was a period when we had actual visions; it was a time of hope for humanity, with people believing that we shaped our destinies. This has long been forgotten. For the most part of the twentieth century, we have lived in the reality of incredible prosperity, in financial terms as well as for the ecosystems. The last 50 years have been radically different, though, and we as a society are on a path of annihilation, with disintegrating societies and declining ecosystems. The question remains, can we break out of this destructive cycle? Can we meet the incredibly important challenge of becoming sustainable?

We have long succumbed to the terror of the markets, that is, the stock markets, and the quarterly profits of big business, things that are outside the realm of life and death. We have delegated and confined the responsibility for what we truly want as a society to these trivial parameters. This current paradigm not only shapes the lives of billions of people but is believed to be inevitable by most- a natural law that can't be bent. The worst form of dictatorship is the one that is held up by this perverted form of economics. People need to shake off the chains of outdated economics that shape their lives. The current economic theory is the slaveholder in this case, as it is what dictates and maintains conditions inside the economy. Why don't people see that these outcomes are not set in stone? Just a few short decades ago, we had a much different way of managing our economy, and we were considerably more successful, as well as happier overall - so why not now?

Since I was a kid, I've had a vision that, one day in the future, we will defeat ignorance and overcome the dark and sinister mysticism that governs much of society, so that we could finally ensure widespread knowledge and enlightenment. It would be a world that would look back at its past as a dark age, one of ignorance, viewing it with disdain and horror and hoping that the shortsighted actions we took would be forever avoided in the future. We are living in a time of severe economic malpractice, based on unsound economic theories that have a wide array of negative consequences for the whole world.

The most significant task of our generation is to overcome this malpractice by understanding the faulty beliefs behind it and learning the fundamental economic concepts to move forward more productively. At the core of the problem of sustainability lies a whole set of zeitgeist ideas that make up what we could call the *paradigm of scarcity*. This is the current modus operandi, which has caused many of the crises we face today, not only environmentally speaking but also in the socio-economic realms. It is only through a cumulative approach that we will have sustainability take its rightful place as a vital cornerstone of our economy. For a society to prosper, we must acknowledge the vast collective wealth at our disposal, while ensuring its sustainability.

In this sense, it is entirely black and white. Either you have a prosperous society with sustainability, an integral part of the equation, or you have a nation of scarcity, with deprived citizens and declining environmental conditions. In the scenario of poverty, we cannot achieve true sustainability, as we will always lack the necessary funds and resources. But, in a genuinely prosperous economic model, we can implement sustainability without these problems impeding us.

I could very quickly have named this book *the scarcity paradigm Vs. The abundance paradigm* - such is the fundamentally oppositional nature of the two ideas of economics. On one side, there is the potential for universal abundance, while on the other lies our current reality - with millions of miserable existences, living hand to mouth, trapped in a system of scarcity that is holding us back collectively. Though, with a simple paradigm shift, we can move away from this wretched system and move towards a world of abundance.

Let there be no misunderstanding about this - our current economic reality is an artificially created state, as the world is full of abundance, but it is our ideas, our software if you will, that are holding us back. The hardware is there, and it has tremendous potential, but our outdated operating system is too primitive. OK, I understand this is a harsh criticism of our current system, but it is mind-blowing to think that just 50 years ago, in the postwar period up until the mid-90s, we were on a path to extreme financial stability and security, but this all changed in just a few decades, and people aren't asking themselves what caused it. How is it possible to have such a shortsighted view of things?

It is mostly due to economics, and the solution is to make a switch from the economics of scarcity to one of prosperity. There is also a fundamental change in attitudes and a shift in our mindset that needs to accompany it, too, which will empower us to see the world as one of prosperity again. It is a substantial change in the belief systems, yes, but it has to be accompanied by a relatively good understanding of our economic systems. Only a combination of these two components will help us escape the financial nightmare we are currently experiencing.

The problem is that we don't have much time. Action is required now. We are up against so many issues that need resolving and fast. Natural catastrophes are piling up, and only a movement that understands the importance of economics will be able to solve these problems and bring about the necessary positive change.

2

TRAPPED IN OLD IDEAS

I THINK the best way to reach an understanding of this social science is to have it explained by someone that understands what ideas to bring forth and what parts will only create confusion and make the topic unnecessarily broad and complex. It can be easily understood if we follow the real history of its development and pay close attention to the crucial points of the evolution of the economy we have today. This added historical context will make it a more enjoyable process, and the overview of past eras will allow us to understand better the contributing factors that got us to our contemporary economic model. We don't need complicated formulas or mathematics. The science of economics is a broad subject that covers many specific areas of the economy. It includes sub-areas that range from very diverse topics, such as the monetary system, to how competition in markets has evolved and how these conditions cause price fluctuations...

We will follow a more exciting path, though.

By getting to the very core of the issue in this way, you will side-step the unnecessary details that are of little interest to most people and gain a far more useful, broad understanding. An analogy could be made here of the economy functioning as a car - with an engine, fuel, a driver, etc. in what is an all-encompassing productive machine designed to fulfill and satisfy the needs of individuals and society. I will refer to this a few times in this book.

We can start with the premise that what is regarded as regulating the principle of economics is *the law of supply and demand.* This principle, applied to economics, relates to the interconnection of human needs and wants and the frequency and efficacy of how they are met. Supply and demand are based on the concept of mutual needs, meaning that, generally, there exist "markets" that will accommodate these needs. These markets can comprise goods and services or the labor market as an example.

We can state that the law of demand works independently of money, meaning that it is not necessary to involve cash for it to function. Money is a tool that certainly eases the exchange and relative pricing of goods, but it is a tool created by humanity. However, there are specific markets where the money is generally not involved - such an example of one of these "markets" is a fundamental element of nature: the mating game. In such a market, the quantity and quality of competitors in each sex and the number of potential mating partners will determine each individual's chance of success. In this sense, the law of supply and demand does apply to all "participants," and it can be used to determine their opportunities for success, depending on many other factors that also shape this "market."

So, coming back to the markets in the economy where goods

and services are traded, their value is calculated by the quantity available and the number of buyers interested. If there are too few goods available, relative to the number of prospective buyers, then their price will increase. Accordingly, in the opposite situation, their price decreases. The variables at play here are the number of goods available and sometimes their quality. These factors generally determine the value of disposable goods, as a shortage of any product in a market will cause the cost of that particular good to rise. In the opposite situation, goods that are abundant, relative to the demand for them, will have their "worth" decrease and their price diminish.

By adding the monetary exchange to the equation, the value of goods will fluctuate until the "clearing price" is reached - the price people are willing to pay. When the "deal" is done, the market worth is established. In this sense, the law of supply and demand forms the foundation of how the free market economy in its current form functions, with market forces determining prices and the monetary system and means of production at the base of it all.

The evolutionary process of economic systems

On the contrary, economic theory is an attempt to explain how the financial system works, how it came into existence, and how to maximize and optimize its outcomes. The critical distinction to be made here is that the economic systems were not "conceived" by the economists. Instead, the economic system came about as the result of an evolutionary process of optimization that started in the cradle of the first civilization, ever-evolving until reaching the complexity we have today.

Through time, the insights and experience of bankers, traders, buyers, and sellers would develop it through extensive trial and error. Over time, with the people involved directly in the actual workings of the trade tools, these advancements would form an evolutionary process that is responsible for the modern system. Economics, which originated as a distinct science only around four centuries ago, started as an attempt to explain the processes, influences, aims, and goals of our society and to optimize these results.

The thing is, though, there were practical people involved in the development of the economy who drew upon their first-hand experience, such as bankers who were optimizing their lending practices based on their insights and relationships with traders. The modern economic and monetary system has developed through many socio-political revolutions and has endured many fundamental failures through time. A prominent example of this is the collapse of the feudal system. The banking system, as well as the monetary system and our means of production, became ever more complex as time went on as a result of economic overhauls as well as socio-political restructuring...

In Europe, since the early Middle Ages, when the first semblance of a banking system emerged, we have seen specialization of lending practices that permitted a higher availability and flexibility of funds, which empowered greater efficiency in the enterprise, as well as corporate co-ownership of entrepreneurial endeavors. In the right context, this would permit the expansion of economic activity through businesses specifically specialized in banking practices with the semblance of a modern financial sector.

The evolution of the monetary tool is commonly believed to have begun with barter or money tokens. Contrary to this common belief, there is evidence to suggest it was mainly done by various methods of recording debits and credits in ledgers. This has been done in some form or other since antiquity and formed the base on which the economy, as we know it, was generally built. Keeping track of such activities eventually came to be known as "bookkeeping" and was done on various materials, recording the exchanges of both debtor and creditor in any transaction. The majority of trade in human history has taken place by tracking such debits and credits.

One example is the tally stick in Europe. This stick was cut in two - one piece representing the debt owed and its counterpart representing a credit claim on the debtor. These sticks could be exchanged and would constitute the first form of *"debt-money,"* which closely resembles how new governmental accounting functions as what is called *"double-entry bookkeeping"* today. In this format, for every credit on one side of the equation, there must be the same sum recorded as a debit on the opposite side. When the debt has been paid, all that remains is the physical goods for the owner, and the entry is canceled. In this sense, such a method is used to allocate real physical assets one possesses, and it is the basis of the debt-money we use today.

While credits and debts were still the basis of trade in the economy in the early middle ages, it was in this period that a florid business in coins of precious metals began. This quickly gained popularity in Europe and resembled the modern money tokens we use for our everyday expenses today. There existed many currencies, with regional variations, even differing from town to town. Can you imagine doing business with 300 currencies in a single state? Not only that, but these coins suffered from extreme price fluctuations and, in some cases, totally lost all worth and were no longer accepted due to the unstable nature and irregular supply of precious metals. The law of supply and demand was not well understood at that time, and these happenings sparked conspiracies and severe punishments when gold coins were not accepted.

The issuers of such coinages ranged from monarchs and land-lords to even the church. They often abused this power by artifi-cially setting and inflating the value of their currencies, often devaluing them when it was beneficial to do so, such as when raising funds for waging wars and other "beneficial" projects. This is where the original idea of *"debasing"* currency originated, which has survived since then, even though, as we will see, it is no longer as applicable and runs contrary to the mainstream ideas.

The first form of money resembling the modern style was issued by private banks and institutions that would have their paper currency and could be redeemed with gold at request in the 17th century.

The most crucial step in the evolution of monetary systems was the inception of a gold-backed currency in the UK in the 18th century, which was a monopoly of the state government and over-took the previous regional system by creating a single, centralized currency. This would be the first of its kind, and the rest of the world soon after adopted similar policies. Private money issued by banks would gradually be abolished in favor of national currencies, with central banks taking on the role of the regulator and guardian of the coin.

It had paper money backed by reserves of gold, and upon request at the central bank, it was guaranteed to be exchanged for its equivalent value of gold at a fixed rate set by the central bank. Such a commodity-backed currency has significant drawbacks; for example, the relative ratio of gold to paper money has to be maintained to maintain the stability of such currency. It is a very inflexible system because, to expand the monetary base for the economy, further gold reserves were needed, and there was, and still is, a finite amount of gold. The contrary is also true as it was undoubtedly susceptible to instability if sudden and substantial gold discoveries were made that endangered the fixed value of gold concerning its supply.

Nevertheless, it was a significant step towards a unified system that would greatly ease trades and transactions and wipe out many of the previous inefficiencies. The advancements in the economic capacity of our societies would enormously accelerate as a result, and our development would progress in increasingly shorter intervals from this time on.

These evolutions, combined with the setting of a common currency, were critical processes in starting the industrial revolution. By setting a single monetary standard, as well as empowering the state as the guardian of the economy with a common currency it controlled, we were able to ease the process of trade and thus stimulate economic activity drastically.

The modern form of money can be regarded as a *"creature of the state"* with governments in place to guarantee the supply of sufficient currency in the economy necessary to ensure markets remain *"liquid"* (guaranteeing ease of exchangeability). This is a vital characteristic in creating a versatile system upon which the modern economy thrives. The central bank provides bank reserves under the same money creation principle described above.

P sum it up, governments were instrumental in putting forward the necessary common purpose, which, quite remarkably, successfully optimized the outcomes to create an efficient financial infrastructure that could support the expansion of economic activity for all.

National currency and laissez-faire policies

The spirit of the time was that of a great revolution, and historically speaking, this would also be a determining factor for the coming into existence of the "nation" as a distinct entity and the emergence of nationalism. Indeed, from the inception of the industrial revolution, around 300 years ago, we saw tremendous development in our means of production, and the wealth it generated began to grow exponentially in correlation.

The realities of such societies in that era brought massive gains in productivity but very slowly translated into widespread prosperity. We instead saw societies with a few rich economic barons and a huge disempowered working class. It that sense, the gains in economic activity and productivity soon ceased to benefit the population as a whole. It is from this period that the classical theories of economics originated, with economists laying out the foundations of what is now known as *classical theory*.

The 18th century was also the cradle of *laissez-faire*

economics, which argued that private individuals should have the most freedom and that government should stay out of the economy, as it would only be a hindrance to individual, private entrepreneurship. The origins of laissez-faire economics were in ideological stances of that period, but it is also worth remembering the limits it stood against were from a time before this new, much more productive economy.

Countless small states that put tariffs on trade in their economy, such as regional barriers, stifled the true potential for the development of trade and greatly reduced potential productivity. The laissez-faire approach was in opposition to these barriers by allowing the breakup of these older, state-controlled monopolies that were seen as little more than a hangover from past eras.

In the same way, the social revolutions that took place in that period popularized the shift away from birth-right rulers, such as a monarchy, towards a competition-based market economy, where wealth was more associated with the domination of economic entrepreneurship. This was becoming the status quo of the elite in society, with business owners and the wealth resulting from their brilliance being idealized and regarded as true economic progress.

Monarchy-driven governments stagnated in the ideas of previous centuries, where kings and monarchs exerted a firm grip on the economy and enacted strict regulations. There were even those who outlawed competition and the free market, for fear that private entrepreneurship would exert more control over the countries in which they operated in than their governments. These were tumultuous times indeed, rife with dramatic social uprisings, such as the French revolution, to liberate societies from the grip of these anti-democratic forces and give control to private organizations in the hopes that more freedom and more prosperity for all would be the result.

While this was a welcome change to help break up older, repressive power structures that were holding back free enterprise and keeping monopolies alive, they made out the enemy to be the state itself. It was clear that the power of a small ruling elite had too much control over the economy and would not tolerate competition. These ideas eventually brought about a release from the monopolies of corrupt governments that were hurting both traders and merchants.

In that sense, laissez-faire economics was a force for good since it removed the limitations imposed by the aristocracy of the time. The main drawback has been that laissez-faire economics assumed that all government action in the economy is bad and should thus be curtailed. It argued against *any* state intervention in markets for fear of repressive government-run monopolies and tariffs returning.

The maxim on which laissez-faire economics is based is to let the market "regulate itself." These ideas, developed by the prominent economist Adam Smith, started the classical era and stated that the "market" would auto-regulate itself; an "invisible hand" would allocate all resources efficiently if left to its own devices. Once the market determines the price, the "participants" in the economy will handle the price on their own, and this is best achieved without laws or regulations imposed by the government, with intervention always being seen as unfavorable and in direct opposition to the theorized market perfection.

The belief here is that a market without laws and regulations would let private actors establish the correct price for goods or wages, lowering or raising costs until a clearing price is established and all participants are satisfied. This is a highly controversial position, though, as we will explore in the following pages.

From gold to paper

The gold standard persisted worldwide until well into the 20th century. Commodity as a base of a currency is not optimal, though, because the lack of scalability in the system leaves it at risk of crashing, which it ultimately did in the currency crisis of the late '6os. Since 1972, all nations dropped the gold-standard, as it became evident that convertibility would not be guaranteed, which made the currencies crash. The gold-standard proved too inflexible to be sufficiently scalable to match the growth of the economy.

Significant turmoil ensued, with the conference of Bretton Woods that brought us to a pure paper money system, called *FIAT money*, which isn't backed by anything other than good faith in the government to guarantee its acceptance, enforced by taxation. This was a massive revolution, as it invalidated the gold-standard logic we had previously relied upon, and we entered a new money paradigm. With it came the extremely flexible system we have today, namely a pure paper money system based on this FIAT money.

The importance of this development was overlooked by many economists who didn't fully grasp the premise of such a radical change. From this date on, the currency would no longer be backed by a commodity to which its "worth" is pegged. From then, currencies would "float," meaning they would be priced against each other and demand for currencies would assign their worth relative to each other. This is how we establish the flexible exchange rates we know today, from the forex (foreign exchange) market.

The paper itself has no "intrinsic" worth, but its acceptance and taxation cause it to be of worth. While I mention paper as the material for money, the majority of cash resides in digitally held bank accounts, with paper money being used only for everyday operations. What is interesting is that, under such a system, we don't encounter any technical limitations on the "money creation" side as we did under a gold-standard system. Money creation under a FIAT money system has no hardwired limit; the central bank can theoretically create as much money as it wishes in its currency.

In a simplified model, it adds numbers in bank accounts when it creates a new currency and subtracts numbers from them when it destroys money. Currency, in its modern form, can be explained with a scoreboard analogy. Governments, with their central banks, are the scorekeepers in the economy, crediting accounts when "creating" money and debiting accounts when money is "destroyed"... From this perspective, the old system of debits and credits with the tally stick becomes problematic, so this is where double-entry accounting comes in handy.

The injection of new money in the economy is done in two ways, first by government spending (with deficit spending) and second when banks loan out bank reserves when the creditworthiness of individuals or firms is established. We could take the car analogy again. Money injection works like a fuel, with a considerable difference, though, that money will be re-spent until it is taxed out or goes into savings.

One thing to keep in mind is that (as a textbook example) the central bank has first to create the new funds in order for banks to loan and government to spend. This invalidates all the logic that is generally accepted as true by most. One of the differences between the two is that spending by the government can be controlled, while bank-loans (given the creditworthiness) will expand and contract depending on the conditions inside the economy.

The mainstream belief in what is called fractional-reserve banking is once more fallacious; they believe that the banking system is lending-constrained and that they first need to have deposits to borrow. MMT has proven that banks will lend if creditworthiness is established, as the central bank will always provide the necessary reserves. Banks, therefore, have unlimited capacity to lend when creditworthiness is established. It is here that the belief in the scarcity of money and gold-standard logic is flawed, as it ignores the fact that the government holds a monopoly and is the sole issuer of currency.

When loans are extinguished, the central bank subtracts the numbers from its books at the central bank, thereby "destroying" the reserves it provided for the banks. While in the past, this was done on actual ledgers by book-keepers, nowadays, it is all done digitally with keystrokes and electronic "wiring." For a system that wants to grow its economy, being held back by the inconvenience of having to come up with more gold reserves is not an option.

Mainstream economists still trapped in ideas of scarcity

Mainstream economics didn't catch up to this extreme change in monetary systems that happened only 50 years ago and is still trapped in the gold-standard mentality. It still relies heavily on private funding by issuing bonds for government spending and is limited by the gold-to-currency ratio. This lack of scalability is no longer a problem, though, due to the implications of the FIAT system.

This gives rise to critical fallacies in theory that don't permit them to see the advantages of the system and, ultimately, the true potential and flexibility of a paper money system. This causes them to assume the scarcity of money is real and tangible. As for debasing the currency, what they call "money printing," it is not tangible, as the intrinsic value of paper money is zero, besides faith in the currency. We will come back to the topic of money creation, inflation, and money printing later in chapter 6.

What you should take from the above paragraphs is that national governments with their respective central banks have the ability to create money out of nothing. They can come up with any new money they want, as they are the monopoly issuers of their respective currencies. This is true for countries like the US, Japan, UK, and many more. It doesn't apply to the Euro though, as they delegated it to a central bank not under their control.

These insights rely on *MMT* (modern money theory), which we covered earlier, and are currently making their way into the mainstream by explaining in a factually correct way the actual workings of the current FIAT money system. The way to under-stand money in general, but more importantly in our unified system, is that money is an accounting tool of a physical counterpart, namely the actual goods and services in an economy, the natural resources available, as well as many other parameters that are "monetized." Economics tries to organize what the real resources of a productive system or nation are through the tool of monetary policymaking.

In this sense, we can say that money drives the economy by being an accounting system for assigning real resources. In short, the money tool is the counterpart to allocate real goods, capital, and resources, and we are no longer constrained by the issuance of the "allocative counterpart" under this new system. It is a tool to allocate resources, to guarantee the fluid workings of trade in society. That is the easy way to understand money as a tool to organize and allocate resources, as well as manage risk and competition.

On that premise, the price, or "price metric," is merely an allocative measure, not an actual "price" to be paid in an "out of system" view - just as meters and kilos are only allocated to measure things and are not the things themselves...

The law of demand determining the price will also automatically stabilize prices, as goods or services that are too abundant will rapidly lose value; for example, if too many monetizable goods, such as houses, are sold at once, this will create an oversupply of houses, which will make the price decline and thus disincentivize many people to sell, creating more stable prices.

To conclude, on the level of production, it took time for the developed economies to establish the current state of efficiency to satisfy the demand of the marketplace. In prior eras, the expansion and efficiency of the production of real goods were limited by the sub-optimal organization of a society, its small-state systems with their tariffs, and the limited knowledge and technology available - all of which would rapidly develop in the course of the last 100 years.

In the same way, the allocative side of the real resources and the money systems developed over time from inelastic, inefficient commodity-backed money and regional currencies. It developed into banks operating on the modern model of paper money, with its scalable money supply and the incredibly efficient clearing mechanisms of the global banking and financial sectors.

All this inflexibility gave rise to bottlenecks of supply, which, in our modern economy, are almost non-existent and in a state of relative balance, something that is reflected in relatively stable prices. All this development would translate into the productive capacity of today, where supply and demand regulate themselves.

Modern economists have inherited the scarcity mindset of the imperfect, suboptimal economic systems of the past and are still trapped in the paradigm of the ineffective tool of monetary creation. They believe in the "scarcity of money" of financial wealth, which we don't suffer from at all under the current FIAT money system - this translates into the current paradigm of "wealth creation" and productivity maximization instead of one focused on effective resource allocation.

Thus, they will try to "squeeze" productivity to the max to reach an ideal state of wealth and will view sustainability and other forms of regulations as simply a hindrance to "wealth creation." Instead of "wealth allocation," most of the profession of economics are stuck in "wealth creation." Their being "stuck" in the inefficiency of the monetary and economic systems of the past remains, despite the many hardwired limits that were successfully overcome. They don't see the system for what it is: the government has the ability to adjust the "temperature" of the monetary part of the economy.

This "mentality of scarcity" of the money token has a chain reaction on the economy as a whole, causing needless destruction to socio-political and environmental aspects of our world. Much of the mainstream economics is trapped in those old systems that had hardwired drawbacks, and this translates into flawed thinking. It has not truly adapted to the system we have now.

The implications of these systemic changes render their prescriptions completely useless or, worse, greatly damaging.

3

THE MYTH OF THE ECONOMIC HERO

As we said, laissez-faire economics argues that the government has no place in the economy, that it should severely limit its influence in the marketplace and its spending, which was extremely low throughout the 19th century. It was in this period that the myth of the "self-made man" originated, giving rise to the idea that only private actors were the sole creators of wealth and economic growth. Also, it was believed that they would put forth the necessary advancements to create and maintain wealthy societies.

While the poverty of early industrialization did reach record highs in the western countries, the conditions throughout the following 19th century were not much better. The same two-class society was in effect, and while economic expansion happened, for the most part, a majority was still living in poverty. Greatly increased productivity did not translate into greater prosperity for all, and the resulting wealth was hoarded in the hands of the few. There were extreme swings in unemployment, as stabilizing factors, such as unemployment benefits, were not yet implemented. So, when crises and recession hit the economy, a great deal of impoverishment for the poorer classes was the result.

The era of the railroad tycoons characterized the considerable gains in productivity through the mass production of the 19th century. They certainly had the vision to build a lot of the infrastructure in the new world but became known for their ruthless indifference to what it would take to achieve it and for their corruption. They grew ever wealthier, while laborers had very different lifestyles of poverty and deprivation of basic human rights. Productivity was the north star to which they looked for guidance, and although there was some legislation governing the exploitation of nature through the pollution from the burning of carbon and the use of dangerous substances, it was still regarded as secondary to the pursuit of prosperity.

This approach that would be forced upon the economy was characterized by the ideas of *individualism*, alongside *Darwinism* - the idea of *"survival of the fittest."* The logic was that, in a free market economy, everyone deserved what they got according to the value they represented in the marketplace. Remember, it was in this time that the myth of the self-made man came into existence - one who could face all adversities in life and win, and he would be considered to be of merit and receive wealth for doing so. For the vast majority that failed though or for those who were born into poverty, a life of hardship was almost inevitable, and such people would be made to feel "guilty" for having poor parents, that is, if they did not abandon them out of economic necessity.

It is this mindset concerning financial wealth in the eyes of economists of the 18th and 19th century that caused one's economic position to carry a moral connotation. Most of the ideas of the time were *Malthusian* in nature - of projecting morals and ideologies onto the economy and applying these moral beliefs to determine how markets "should" operate. They projected those values onto the market participants as individuals. For example, forced trivial moral "values" of merit and beliefs in the inferiority of poor people, branding them as lazy and incapable of taking care of themselves, emerged at this time. It was actually theorized that poor people should stay in poverty as, otherwise, they would engage in vices and other damaging behavior. It was a greatly patronizing approach.

By bringing these ideas into the economy, they effectively created many of the conditions we still see today. These ideas went to become deeply ingrained within our society for reasons that we will get into in this chapter. This self-imposed moral approach brings about a black or white scenario of a minority of successful people and a majority that live their lives in poverty. It is a competition that forces an unequal division - some winners and many losers, with a mix of Darwinism and religious moralism at its core. In the society they envisioned, it would be extremely difficult to rise out of poverty.

The myth of the self-made man translated into the idea that these actors were the true bringers of economic prosperity for society. Some made a fortune, though the majority did not. It was simply not a decent society as far as standards of living across all sections of society were concerned, as the masses barely survived and had little to no hope of retirement or escaping this poverty. Concepts such as labor or environmental protection were not even considered under this system. The same can be said for the European factories and their exploitation of workers. These were an exact antithesis of a prosperous middle-class society, with conditions in these factories having disastrous effects across society.

The rights revolution

Towards the end of the 19th century, a transition towards a more inclusive society began with anti-elitist sentiments becoming popular, and an equal society that took inspiration from the enlightenment of the French Revolution and the American Bill of Rights beginning to take shape. This all culminated in the rights-based societies of the twentieth century.

In this climate of ideas, oriented towards a more inclusive society, a natural development of liberation for the inferior parts of society in their continuous states of deprivation and poor working conditions began. This brought to the forefront the common interests of the working classes, and through political activism, in the middle of the 19th century, the first rebellions occurred, culminating in an outright fight for rights and improvement of working conditions.

They organized unions, which started to force politicians to act in a way that would more fairly distribute the productivity that only went to the top 1% of the time. This was encountered with great hostility, as it threatened the interests of the economic elites, which was intertwined with the interests of the political elites. The labor unions that formed in the mid-19th century gained considerable political power into the start of the last century and revolutionized society. They brought gradual improvement to working conditions and created worker's rights, all of this contrary to the worldview of the "culpability" of being poor that was seen in the 18th century.

The ideas of laissez-faire economics were relegated, and a more government neutral approach became standard - the sentiment was that the government should assist the society in reaching its goals but not define them. It was in the first part of the 20th century that a significant revolution took place, one that was arguable to economics what the Copernican revolution was to astrophysics. The economist Maynard Keynes revolutionized economic theory after two centuries of laissez-faire policies. Laissez-faire, while advancing the productive output of the country, did ultimately fail to create real prosperity, as the two classes of society and the extreme disparity of rich and poor were still a hard reality.

Keynesianism was the antithesis of the laissez-faire stance of restricting the government to only strictly necessary action in the economy. The insights were that markets inevitably tended to disrupt themselves and that government action, and more importantly its spending, would not only prove to be a tremendous stabilizing force in the economy but that it would counterbalance the recessive periods. Keynes saw that classical economics failed to deliver real prosperity, and one of the main reasons for this was the ideological stance of restricting the government from assisting in shaping favorable conditions for the economy to operate within.

Counterbalancing the boom and bust-cycles highlighted the need to break the short-circuit of liquidity. When this happened, unemployment would rise, and so it was argued that the government should do what was necessary to make the economy restart a new, more successful cycle. One reason for the economy entering periods of recession is that bank loans, which made up the huge majority of the money in the economy, would cause it to go bust. As soon as it became clear that a downturn was approaching, banks would cut back borrowing and make it an inevitability.

These cycles would only become more extreme because the banking sector tended to overexpose itself in boom cycles and immediately cut back in bust cycles, drying up liquidity in the system. The idea that there was a need for a dominant player to be decisive and make the economy thrive when it entered recessive periods was regarded as the mainstream way to go. The government is the only player able to break the cycle, as human psychology would make people wary of spending when the outlook was negative.

In today's mainstream policy, the current prescription is that adjusting monetary policy, namely the adjusting of interest rates, is the best option and that lowering interest rates will spark more loans. This will result in more injection of financial wealth to revive the economy; therefore, contrary measures should be taken during boom cycles. This position has been disproved in the last decades since interest rates have slipped towards zero, and there has not been any considerable recovery in sight for the middle class, even though the stock market has enjoyed record highs.

It is clear by now, even to many in the mainstream, that fiscal policy (government spending/taxation) is the only tool to bring about acceleration to the economic motor during recessions. Central banks have used up all the tools they had at their disposal to encourage lending, but the propositions are wrong. Monetary policy is only useful under regular conditions to adjust the "temperature" of the economy, not to escape recessions. Only fiscal policy will work. The government, with its firepower in the form of spending, is the only force that can actively counterbalance when the motor grinds to a halt, resulting in a market economy that naturally leans toward dysregulation by the many behaviors of its participants.

Government interventionism in the imperfect market

Government spending, being low to non-existent under laissez-faire thinking, rose throughout the 20th century.

In the first part of the 20th century, with the effects of World War One, government spending skyrocketed as nations were dedicated to the war, meaning that, from now on, the government, with its spending, would become a key player in the economy. The great depression signified the end of the belief of the perfection of the free market left to its own devices, as was theorized by the classical economists, and this abruptly halted a relatively long period of economic expansion. Staggeringly high rates of unemployment meant the ruin of many lives, and the tales of the harsh conditions of those times have come to be known in many movies and books.

It was clear that the idea of the "unregulated market" correcting itself was wrong. With many economic participants being unemployed, it would be incapable of the recovery it needed - the cycle of spending, business investments, and labor wages saw the doctrine of the "free market" crumble under the evidence of reality. Markets crashed and took the majority of jobs with them, causing extreme suffering.

The misery resulting from all of this brought about the concept of growing expenditures made by governments to ease the peoples' suffering and to break the cycle of the economic quagmire. Government involvement in the economy through stabilizing action was welcomed then. This brought on global initiatives, such as in the US, with its "New Deal" from President Roosevelt and similar experiments elsewhere that created government programs of investing in the economy and wealth redistribution through wage negotiation. Government spending went from below 2% in the year 1900 to far higher figures in World War II (WW2), which signified a huge expense and a rise of 60% in GDP ratio made by the government to fund the wars.

In WW2, significant investments were made by the government for the development of industries to satisfy the need for instruments and armaments. During the war, the spending ratio to GDP produced was at 40%. This forced investment through the war effort from the government fostered the creation of new industries that continued to be successful in the post-war years and resulted in the record growth and prosperity of the post-war period. The skyrocketed spending, together with the societal pact between social classes that were fought by the workers' organizations, proved successful in paving the road to prosperity. Productivity finally translated into widespread prosperity by the conditions set and negotiated and their resulting profit redistribution. Government spending proved instrumental in providing the fertile ground for favorable economic development.

It proved a stabilizing factor for the economy, as it used spending in the economy to fund unemployment benefits once the economic cycle crashed to stabilize consumer spending. This sort of spending stimulated businesses to reinstate laborers and bring the economic motors back online. In mere economic terms, we can say that injecting funds will "make the car go faster." Generally speaking, by injecting funds, one way or another, the consequences will be that automatically people will spend more money in the economy, and more products will be sold. Using the spending power of the government to regulate the system will result in price stability, as full employment is good for the economy, whereas political turmoil caused by chronic unemployment is always bad for the economy. When we are at full speed, we will have full employment too, as the majority of products will be sold and the people will be employed.

In recessive periods, when the rates of taxation decreased and the expenditures of the stabilizers rose (unemployment- and other benefits), a bottleneck-scenario was encountered. The government used its stabilization to counteract and restart a new economic cycle. This is the main failing of the classical school of thought- the idea to compare the state to a household, with income determining spending. The incredibly important difference here is that the government is not subjected to taxation to spend as a household would be subjected to income. A state is the sole issuer of its currency, thus is not spending constrained under the FIAT system.

Governments have a monopoly on the issuing capacity of

their currency, so it doesn't work to view the government like a household, which can only spend if it has the money or has to cut it if the income shrinks. Governments have the capacity for money creation *at-nihilo* (out of nothing), so they are not subject to taxation. On a federal level, a government spends first and taxes later. I know this sounds crazy, but if you think carefully, it is true!

One reason mainstream economics is so against government spending is the misplaced belief that it is only the private sector that creates all wealth. It is believed that the government merely benefits from the fruits "created" by the private sector, and government action in the economy only takes resources away from it. The belief here is that government spending through taxation will "crowd out" (take away) financial resources to be spent back in the economy by the private sector. This is completely fallacious thinking since the government doesn't compete for money. It can create money at any time through deficit spending when taxes are not enough to match expenditures.

They argue that the government will compete for money with the taxes, so their natural conclusion is the proposal of cutting government spending. The thing is that the government is the sole player that can break this rule, as it can create money at any time by money creation out of nothing, without the need for tax revenue to fund it. What is clear is that a government should carefully evaluate how to spend money in the economy, as there are hardwired limits; thus, inflationary pressures can arise. Let's leave this topic for now, though, as we will come back to it later.

The government spending of funds in the economy is done by buying products and services from the private sector, as well as by paying for services, such as pensions, and stabilizers, such as unemployment funds. The reality of the last decades has been a lack of spending in the economy. It was particularly true in recessions, such as 2008, when it was shown that the countries that engaged in government spending came out of the crisis faster than those who did not. On the other hand, countries that were involved in austerity, which was cutting spending to get out of a recession, such as Europe, suffered. While Europe was hit much worse, the US used government spending to counterbalance the lack of spending, as well as being a last resort for the banks that overexposed - "bailing out the banks," and it recovered much faster.

By not being constrained by the confines of taxes, the government can help remove these imbalances. Not only that, we will see in later chapters that government spending is the private sector's surplus, as the sectoral balances show us that one's deficit is another's surplus. Therefore, government spending should always be done to accommodate all the basic needs of society, such as correctly functioning roads, hospitals, etc. It should also be used to provide the private sector with the needed financial resources to get out of market failures.

Ideology versus market realities

Unfortunately, ideology has a significant grip on mainstream economics, as they still idealize the "free" market and the private entrepreneurs "creating" all the wealth. We will prove throughout this book that we can manage and "create" the conditions in the market that will give rise to the society that we want, without sacrificing rights or environmental regulations. While the private actors are certainly needed, they are actors in the game, not directors. The idea that we are dependent on the "private sector" to create jobs is only part of the story and does not include the government action to create the necessary ground to thrive on. All players are needed to aim for prosperous conditions and shape the society that we have in mind.

We don't need to get "saved" by "self-made men" to provide us with economic wealth. Entrepreneurs certainly have their place in the importance of the economy, but there never was a lack of them. If we suddenly have a lack entrepreneurship in a niche and a void is created, private actors will fill it to accommodate demand, generally speaking. Of course, there have been revolutionary entrepreneurs, and these have sped up the development of the economy in recent times. That has been their significant contribution in the short period of growth, achieving the efficiency of today.

The private sector, as a whole, is pretty much capable of coming up with solutions to satisfy demand; we don't need to rely on "*McDonald's*" for food or "*Apple*" for mobiles. The cornerstone of a market economy is that enough competition created by the law of demand will create the supply. So, by the nature of competition, the "best" will be brought to the top, and this is the case of the economy: if one business fails, it will be followed by another that may be more successful. It is again the interweaving of supply and demand that guarantees an adequately deep market. So, the whole discourse that we need to take care of the businesses is ridiculous, and the best way to have all the players involved, thriving, is not to drain the liquidity out of the system.

We could also argue that it is in national interest to have competitive industries and to have some supply guaranteed, to not depend on monopolies. What is not in the interest of each country is the idea that we need to obsess about ever-increasing productivity to have enough jobs in the economy, in a "private sector creates all jobs" paradigm. The government needs to provide the prosperous ground on which to thrive carefully, or we will slip into the "jobs creation" myth, which under the current conditions is starved liquidity.

The myth of "the private sector creating all the wealth" is a false assumption propagated by the same people that do not understand economic principles and the realities of the modern economy. You will find a lot of propaganda from this huge crowd that has been indoctrinated by the universities to think of the economy in this way. So, it is not surprising that almost all commentators in the media and politics still push forth a concept of advantaging the "supply-side," which is the idea that businesses have a special place in the economy compared to "consumers" and "laborers" so we should favor them and guarantee advantages to them. The right balanced way is to consider each market participant in the same way, be it consumer, laborer, or business, as each is important in the economic engine. Favoring one with favorable conditions will disadvantage the others and cause an imbalance in the economic motor.

Now it is clear that burdening businesses with excessive taxation will hinder their ability to pay wages, so it should be done according to what we want to see in the economy and in a progressive manner, which is a further stabilizing factor as we will see later in the book. The idea that businesses should not go broke at all is wrong. It is part of the competition-based economy that we have, where the better outcompetes the less efficient, and this will result in a more productive system. The bigger reason that we are in such dire straits, economically speaking, is clearly due to starved liquidity.

The evidence suggests that, if we shape the conditions within the economy, the private sector will thrive. So, contrary to today's belief, government spending would spur the highest economic growth in the history of humankind and the most prosperous period! The reality shows that moralizing against poor people by smearing them as lazy and undeserving is not useful. All while there is evidence in this world that poverty generates further poverty, and prosperity drives people towards success. Stigmatizing poor people, engaging in heavy mystification, and idealization of such values as who is "deserving" only creates a polarized society of more impoverished neighborhoods and wealthier neighborhoods. Stigmatization like this goes against the massive evidence base that - if given the right conditions, generally, social mobility will happen.

There have been studies that have even shown that randomly giving out money to people in need, such as universal basic income experiments, created radically better outcomes than the poverty assistance provided today and in a shorter period. All the evidence points towards poverty as a cycle and wealth being the same. This is in stark contrast to the bullshit you hear about the "takers" and the lazy people from certain political parties that are interested in keeping things the way they are. A lot of the poor people are not limited because of "laziness" but because they lack the money to initiate their way out of poverty and into prosperity. This should be common sense.

Evidence proves that a prosperous economy is a result of sharing profits and that the gains of one individual do not have to be counterbalanced by the losses of another. The spending by one individual will make up the gains of the lack of spending by another. So then, the government should try its best to help the weakest in the chain, as they will, in turn, contribute to someone else's prosperity. Punishing people for being poor will not make things better. It makes matters worse, and the belief of them being lazy is just further insult and an irrelevant attempt to push flawed moral values upon other people.

In prior centuries, they had no understanding that the successful economy was based upon a sharing principle. To have widespread prosperity in society is hardly accomplishable if we punish people that don't "merit" wealth - especially if we project religious/moral values upon them. A parallel here can be drawn with ideas such as slavery that are now contrary to today's laws. It can be said that human rights were hugely profitable for all. To create wealth, you need to have individuals that use their worth and wealth as an individual and their spending to make up for others less fortunate. In this sense, a robust and prosperous economy is one of sharing my resources and qualities for your benefit. The propaganda of an ideological position of cutting government spending without creating other ways of injecting money will inevitably drain liquidity from the economy and render the reality of the majority of working people even harder. Continuing to do this is quite simply contrary to the evidence and will only further starve the system and create unemployment.

While the "crowding out" of financial wealth is plainly a myth, the crowding-out effect does happen on the physical side of the economy, so government spending is not always the optimal way to make up the liquidity in the system, as it competes for real resources. I will argue later in this book that we should instate a third way of money creation, which will further help to stabilize the system, and it will function as a further cushion to provide liquidity for the system, reducing some drawbacks resulting from government overspending.

Again, the approach should be one of "functional finance" and, rather than obsess about accounting practices, we should aim for outcomes that we wish to see. As an example, remember earlier in the book when we discussed how we had actually followed full employment policies in the twentieth century, right up to the eighties? It was a prosperous time, though we have since left that path to have good aims shape good outcomes, based on the common mantra of our times being, "We can't afford it!" In this sense, it was a period when we had actual visions; it was a time of hope for humanity, with people believing that we shape our destinies - this has long been forgotten.

By contrast, the aims and ideals of the ideologies of scarcity will reach a perfect state of poverty. We can plan these "markets" so that the outcomes are pretty much foreseeable, based on the "prescriptions" upon which they are based. The underlying conditions that are set by laws and regulations shape the environment inside the market. If favorable underlying conditions are created by state intervention, this, in turn, will create the "market ecology" to thrive on. Moral principles do not apply to economics, in the same way that the central bank canceled trillions of dollars of bad debt that resulted from the banks not doing their job properly by overexposing during the last great financial recession. The central bank took on the debt, and guess what, it simply canceled it from their books.

4

AN EXPLOITATION DOCTRINE

I N THE EIGHTIES, laissez-faire economics was revived by the Reagan and Thatcher-administrations after 50 years of Keynesianism, when the crisis of inflation that emerged in the 70s could not be brought under control and explained by Keynesian economists. This brought with it the old ideas of aversion to government intervention and the plan that removing all limitations in the market economy would transport us into the promised land of prosperity again. We would enter an era of free-market doctrine with an economy of global trade becoming a reality.

The ideas of the primacy and the perfection of markets without regulations, laws, and barriers were brought to the mainstream and have since been the pillar of political action, without awareness of much of the impact it has on the population. It was the result of collective efforts by interested groups and economic elites, which in turn enjoyed spectacular results and record profits. It has also been a reality that, while the elites were making these record profits that have continually risen in the last 50 years, the prosperous middle classes have declined. This has been an effort to implement extreme classism again.

The idea is that, by benefiting the businesses and the upper classes in the form of tax cuts, it will automatically help the laborer as well since it is assumed that money would "trickle-down" to them as well in the form of increased investment and thus wages. These prescriptions have been adopted worldwide by most governments in the last 50 years. It is doubtless that this thinking is soaked in ideology and morals with no evidence to back it up. All evidence suggests that wealth will be hoarded, with money ending up in tax havens or driving up housing prices and the stock market, which has reached unbroken record highs in recent years, while the mainstream is hurting.

The thing is that evidence suggests that not only is it not working, but the contrary is also happening - money trickles upwards, making a few billionaires richer while the huge majority feels a small or negative effect. This is also problematic from an ethical point of view - that it will trickle down to "the poor classes" as it violates a sharing and human rights principle of the proven prosperous economy of prior decades. It is this approach that has been the main reason for poor economies, with them being continually hit by recessions, and people not managing to make ends meet even though they are overworked. Looking at it objectively, the rat race and the overexploitation of workers have resulted in a health crisis of overstressed people with symptoms like burnout being much more common.

Inequality has skyrocketed with a small minority of individuals owning more than the bottom 50% of the population combined, and you don't hear much from the press or the main-stream economists about this. To make things worse, the growing disparity also drives up prices for "the poor people" as purchasing power on the side of the upper classes influences costs. The economy that has been established through policy is wrong on any level - human happiness, ethical, economical and systemic, with inequality posing a threat to democracy. What has been willfully enforced is an economy of over-competition where inequality is practically wished for, as it is theorized that it furthers the goal of productivity and is "making us all rich".. and therein lies the fallacy.

Incentivizing competition and inequality to increase productivity paired with cutting government spending is a perfect way to cripple liquidity in the system, as more productivity makes the motor more efficient and further drains liquidity due to the loss of jobs. We may say this has been a purposeful reinstatement of the oligarchy economics of prior eras by the billionaire class, as it has proved immensely profitable to them.

Regression instead of progression

The ideological removal of market stabilization combined with a deliberate crippling of the liquidity present in the economic systems by austerity has brought us to the current nightmare scenario of mass unemployment and economic hardship for the masses. The original idea of laissez-faire by the early economists was one that proposed unregulated markets and the restraint of government or organizations from regulating it to apply the principle of supply and demand without any filter. This, therefore, was stating that it was better if the market participants were left alone to handle the price increasing or decreasing until the market worth was established and the "clearing the price" was reached when the people were willing to pay it.

This is where their idealism of the perfection of the free market goes wrong, and they will argue that the price clears best when there are no barriers, such as governmental laws and regulations, in place - hindering minimal conditions of wages and the prices of goods and services, welfare conditions, and safeguards in the economy. This belief is utopian at best and dangerous at worst. Prices cannot be lowered endlessly, since it will gravely infringe on safety and/or human well-being. When there are no regulations and laws in place guaranteeing certain conditions, it is guaranteed that, due to human nature, these infringements will happen as history proves.

Not only that, but the idea that, if you lower the price to a certain point, it will have an impact on the interests of businesses and, in turn, on the wages of the people, which will not permit the necessary volume of trade for full employment. It will interrupt the economic cycle as it will bring about recessions. Thus, the system will become dysregulated. The fallacy lies again at the spending part, assuming more growth and productivity can solve our problems of financial scarcity. Prescriptions of austerity paired with deregulation force us into a downward-spiraling economy. There seems to be a "hole" in the system that mysteriously sucks out wealth, making the system poorer and poorer.

And to add insult to injury, when the approach is not working, the answer has been that we haven't tried hard enough, so unemployment programs will be slashed to force people to take up whatever jobs, no matter how low the wage or how bad the conditions. As the system gets poorer and poorer, they still propose the same failed actions - cutting government spending and removing financial, environmental, and labor-regulations, stating that they are holding us back from reaching wealth. Due to the ideological removal of market stabilization such as this and a deliberate draining of the liquidity present in the economic systems by austerity, there are swarms of unemployed people that are desperate to get any job, and the resulting financial insecurity will make people act accordingly. The huge unemployed masses are chasing insufficient jobs, as well as wages that are exposed to the law of demand. This will worsen the downward spiral. Too many laborers seeking too few jobs will put downward pressure on the wages and working conditions. This should be clear to anyone.

In the last twenty years, workers' wages have stagnated, which, of course, translates into less money in the economy to spend, while many media commentators still propose the big fear of inflation. Deflation is the issue, as we are running the economy chronically under capacity for the last few decades, which, of course, translates into the current plague of unemployment or underemployment, as there is not enough trade to guarantee full employment.

Workers without rights

The reality is that, under the current job market, workers don't have much room to negotiate their wages and working conditions as unemployment is high, and they are desperate to get a job.

Therefore, they have very little leverage. Taking away job security due to the fallacious belief that "we need more productivity" has been instrumental in the creation of an economy of precarious jobs, with low-pay and part-time schedules making up a big chunk of the official statistics as employed - even though they get paid under a living wage and don't have "full time" hours. They show in the statistics as employed, even though they can barely sustain themselves.

Through this kind of job, their creditworthiness will inevitably be severely limited by the banks, thus limiting the new injection of money through bank loans into the economy. There is a shortage of opportunities for decent-paying jobs for unskilled laborers. Here the mantra has been that only in-demand qualifications or specializations will save you from ending up with poor choices and opportunities. While it is undoubtedly true that education can better your chances, if fifty persons are applying for a job and only ten positions are available, some will have to suffer unemployment. The problem lies at the spending part on the economy, as too few spending will inevitably cause unemployment.

Coming back to the labor market, on the contrary, if there is a shortage of laborers for a specific job in a market, companies will compete for the laborers, and this may drive up wages and working conditions. Conversely, if there is an abundance of applicants, the employers will choose who they believe will provide them with the best service and dictate the terms freely. We have in place the position of mainstream economics that they call the "natural rate of unemployment" at 5%, which means they see it as unavoidable. It is believed that between 4.5% and 5% of the population will be unemployed at all times for reasons such as automation, so they consider the population at full employment when it is at this rate.

They further reason that minimum-wage policies and unions are interfering with this "natural rate," thus causing more unemployment. It is also the official position that they will use unemployment as a guard against inflation, stating:

"The only way an economy could have a zero percent unemployment rate is if it is severely overheated. Even then, wages would probably rise before unemployment fell to absolute zero."

Even considering some of the validity of the first two reasons, these numbers are staggering if you think that, at 5% unemployment, politicians will see the criteria of full-employment as being met. I'm not making this up; this is currently the official position of economists and politicians alike. They argue all this with phrases like "stock of unemployed" to refer to the unemployed, which is tremendously insulting if you ask me.

This is the reality of the abhorrent ideology of neoclassical economics, which has a clear discriminatory intent towards those less fortunate. Astonishingly, economists can get away with calling people a "stock of unemployed." It shows their contempt towards the so-called "lower classes" and their judgmental approach towards the economy in general. Tell it to all the miserable people that can't get a job — not to mention the high numbers of involuntarily underemployed.

The productivity myth

Less demand and less money to spend at their disposal will lead to consumers in need of lower prices and will inevitably force producers to compete for increasingly lower costs, due to this loss of purchasing power. It will translate into producers having their profit margin decreased and creating a self-sustaining, vicious cycle of chasing lower and lower prices.

Added wealth creation by more productivity was also transferred to the working people some time ago. However, in today's right-less economy, the bonuses go to the stockholders or the managing board. Their "cure" of more productivity will further the problem of too little liquidity in the system and will worsen these conditions, as more productivity makes the system produce more at lower costs, thus furthering the pressure on laborers' wages and spending in the economy.

We have reached the boundaries of productivity in what humans and animals can take, as this race to the bottom is making us all sick and tired of what we feel in our everyday lives. In such a system of getting poorer in every cycle, what remains is that only a growth of the economy can expand the financial wealth in the economy. Thus, this dogma that "we need more growth" that you hear continually by media, economists and politicians is a necessity of sustaining the system by counteracting shrinking liquidity due to their failed prescriptions.

We could sum up this mess by describing it as a perfect vicious cycle scenario.

You would not believe it is possible to look at the data, which shows all negative signs over the past few decades, and still propose over and over again more austerity, more privatization, and tax cuts for the wealthy. The fun fact is that the free-market doctrine has taken on a form of "religious dogma" adopted by almost all the mainstream parties, media, and the economic establishment.

How is it possible to continue with policies that have clearly been shown not to work? Maybe, just maybe, we should try something different (sarcasm intended). Einstein gave a good definition of madness when he said that doing the same thing over and over again and expecting different results is indeed madness. The sad thing is that it is pervasive in almost all universities that teach this wall-street brand of economics. So, you have crowds of indoctrinated people repeating over and over again the absurdities that they have been force-fed, even though they don't correspond to the reality of the economic system.

We should not lose sight of the financialization of government policies and the fact that they have benefited almost exclusively what we call the "economic elites" and wall-street based interests of the financial sector, which are becoming more and more decoupled from the real economy. The financialization of the economy has been a further step in that direction, namely looking at trivial economic indicators, such as the stock market or the sales of multinational corporations, and declaring by that same data that the economy is doing great if they had a successful quarter. All while ignoring the incredible numbers of unemployed and the heavy struggling of a shrinking middle class. Indicators such as taking a functional approach with the aim of full employment and setting the economic aims have been completely abandoned in the last 50 years, with the mantra of the free market deciding what is and what isn't a laudable goal. We are at the mercy of these ideologies and the resulting dysregulated markets that create great havoc and have created an economy of the strictly necessary.

A car without a driver comes to mind.

Global trade in down-spiraling markets

With globalization, which has been a phenomenon that started centuries ago, the reality of worldwide trade has become a reality. The same free-market doctrine has thus been enforced world-wide, and it brings in unlimited competition from economic participants in a globally unregulated market. While globalization is not a bad thing, and the globalization of cultures has been a reality and even a desirable outcome through technology and innovation, trade without barriers in worldwide markets without safeguards in place to guarantee a minimum of safety, rights, and environmental regulations is wreaking havoc.

The proposal is that worldwide markets with such down-spiraling economies and without any laws or regulations or any attempts to stabilize the market conditions will create a wasteful world-economy. This is a reality right now. Unsurprisingly, it will create an environment where the lesser cost and quality will win out. The idea of depotentiation of the state with all the deregulation has been actively put forth by the huge multinational corporations that colluded with politicians, as it would benefit them directly. What we have seen is that these big corporations have become so powerful that their synergistic efforts can often compete for power with their governments. The question of special interests having a huge influence over the political process means that it is no wonder that you see the huge sums that are spent on lobbying. This is a reality in many countries, even more so globally, since the trade agreements are forced upon the world trade.

The way free-market economics was conceived was the most useful ideology for board managers and stockholders alike. It goes hand in hand with more inferior consumer security, especially in a political environment where they heavily influence the decisions to be made.

The big shark economy

It guarantees profits at the expense of several consequences that will impact society negatively - the suppressed state that doesn't ensure regulations against being poisoned by products or manufacturing processes. The prominent players in the industries don't want environmental regulations because they would have to fund them and create safe and sustainable products. This would mean sharing part of their profits. It is that simple.

It fits very well within the short-sighted economics of today, and the economic elites have founded a business model based on corruption that will guarantee these political administrators' well-paid jobs after finishing their political favors. The political corruption is being carried out in the open, with fees paid for speeches in the sum of hundreds of thousands of dollars after their political career.

And indeed, this did play well. These same companies and the billionaires that lead them have endorsed and funded many think tanks that actively put forth the propaganda of "free market ideas," and their "investment" has certainly paid. Let us call it what it is: "depotentiation of the regulations for profit." There, I have it corrected for you. It is common practice by all the foremost corporations to pay for these things as a tacit agreement that everybody has to contribute for lobbying purposes so the big sharks can have a greater profit-margin.

The lobbying does not end at national borders, and it has targeted the financial systems of almost all nations. It has over-taken the WTO, the trading organization, and the various govern-ments that have put forth trading agreements written by hand from the lobbyists to guarantee the continuity of deregulation on a global scale, to maximize profits at the expense of global conditions.

These transnational corporations have put in place laws through their political players to have global access to markets at favorable conditions, and multinational corporations will pick out the most favorable terms from various nations competing for production, as well as for taxation.

Moreover, this cartel of financial power and the interests of transnational corporations in a globalized economy that intrinsi-cally run on profit maximization has brought on the behavior of competition between these multinational companies - all in a race to migrate their production to countries where there are fewer restrictions and regulations to safeguard the environment and labor.

Countries with fewer regulations are winning out in this race towards the bottom, and they will suffer the resulting environ-mental catastrophes. We are seeing this happening in most of the production hubs of the world, in developing countries such as

Bangladesh, China, India, etc. It is common practice for big companies to set their "fiscal headquarters" in financially advantageous countries. They produce the most waste, use all the infrastructure, and pay little in taxes, while smaller companies have to pay the standard rates. Small actors have to comply with the rules, as do individuals. We, therefore, have a big shark economy, where they have corrupted the system and perpetuated a way of being that benefits them, but that does not benefit us the small fish.

I'm not proposing the abolition by the law of more prominent corporations. Instead, what I'm suggesting is that we should not favor a process of multi-nationalization of the economy, as this will stifle competition and create monopolies. Of course, there is a need for some big corporations, but we have reached a model where these large corporations are corrupting the political process to their benefit and are sucking up all the competition from lower businesses, as they cannot compete.

You can see this development in the whole economy, with bigger players removing the small stores at the corner of the street. Now, this didn't happen by chance; it is the conditions and laws that have facilitated this development. I'm also not proposing that we should subsidize unsuccessful or obsolete business models, but I'm arguing in favor of applying these insights when shaping trade laws to guarantee fair competition.

By creating these huge sharks in the economy that can outcompete states, it is forcing laws and regulations on us all to profit their shareholders and board managers. Do we want this kind of economy? It is a big-business economy that does not benefit the mid-sized or small companies that are generally held more accountable. We have been left in a world where these big companies dictate what is right and wrong, based on their profitability. This model of worldwide trade, in a downward-spiraling economy, only aggravates these problems and worsens its symptoms on a global scale. The perception of a lack of wealth in the developing countries is even more problematic than in the "richer" countries, as they need to survive with fewer means, and there is a great deal of corruption going on, with even fewer regulations and less enforcement of those they do have.

That's one reason big corporations prefer to relocate, as they can fully maximize their profits with fewer consequences and ignore environmental catastrophes and the resulting suffering in these countries. Competing in a global market will drive prices to the bottom in the rich nations and will drive up prices in poorer nations, as they all compete in the worldwide marketplace where business goes to the lowest bidder. The developing countries are able to compete more effectively for prices due to the troublesome reality of less stringently enforced regulations and safeguards for their environments. This leads to incredible amounts of waste as the products being manufactured are almost the same, and though the local products are fresher, they go unsold.

In global trade, the fewer laws and regulations governing it, the more damage is caused to the environment, and the more labor is exploited.

5

MONETIZING OF NATURE

THE INEFFICIENCIES of the prevailing economic theory have not taken into account the integrity of the environmental reality, and those who reap the profits will do little to counterbalance this chronic impact because they lack any real incentive to do so under the current free-market paradigm. There are widespread practices of wastefulness that impact carbon footprints, combined with overproduction and unsustainable manufacturing practices.

At the base of this lies the kind of economy we have outlined so far in this book - the approach of the scarcity mindset and the need to create wealth and discharge costs on the ecosystems. Businesses that have to increase profits in quasi-deflationary markets that will encounter extreme difficulties, so what remains is more productivity, which is at the maximum already, while discharging the costs of which onto the environment The reality is that, in this world, you could put a price tag on almost anything - which is why rare animals get trafficked. And it happens in great numbers. For example, the wildlife trade is booming, causing huge damage to ecosystems -people do this to create a living for themselves, and they will do anything to survive.

Such an expansion of "tradable" things may bring some financial wealth, but it comes at a heavy price by destroying the natural world and any hope of sustainability. The market raises profits and passes these costs to the environment, thus, ultimately onto the communities who inhabit them. This shirking of the consequences of this inefficient organization of the economy has a long tradition, and since the inception of industrialization, we have gone down this road. In an idealistic economic scenario, profits are created without impacting the *"future ability"* - there would be enough of a profit margin for all not to engage in what we could class as the monetization of nature, namely the transformation of real ecosystems into financial wealth and destroying them in the process.

We can create financial wealth, but we can't recreate the ecosystems once they are gone. Therefore, we need to move from a paradigm of wealth creation towards wealth allocation, which is ultimately what the money system is supposed to accomplish. By having an economy of sustainable goods and services, as well as allocating them more sustainably, wealth administration would become a reality.

The question may come up here that, if we severely limit supply, it will inevitably impact price stability. I think it is doable; we can overcome the endless growth paradigm and move into a more administrative mode of economics, without creating poverty. Understanding the system itself as being the cause of the problem is crucial here, and we can overcome it without breaking the system. The whole idea of laissez-faire economics and its aim to constrain governments in its original role of regulators of society is coming to an end. Letting markets determine their outcomes or even the "customers with their purse" is outdated, with images of the disastrous results getting more and more prominent every day.

The complete lack of a cheap but sustainable or reusable concept for most products or biodegradable alternatives has had a hugely negative impact on the environment due to the cheaper but unsustainable alternatives being favored by profit-driven corporations. The case for single-use, throw-away products is no longer viable if we don't add biodegradability or if we don't have a realistic concept of a product being reusable at least. This includes the huge quantity of packaging from cartons to single-use plastics, which are not biodegradable, as well as all sorts of foam and so on. The majority of all products are in this category and do not have a product afterlife. They will mostly end up polluting the environment or burned in incinerators, ending up as emissions, creating an enormous hazard for wildlife and generations to come. This isn't sustainable.

The plastic disaster is getting worse, literally every minute. If we don't act promptly, there will soon be more plastics than fish in the oceans. The free-market theory of how to resolve this issue is that consumers should choose not to buy plastics when shopping. The reality is that there is often no other option; almost all goods are packaged in plastic as it is cheaper to do it this way. The true "price" of plastic is that it takes 1000s of years to decompose. Why would you put out products that take 100s if not 1000s of years to break down? And it only breaks down into smaller particles, I must add. The huge waste that will result from a short-lived, single-use product will increase over time.

Just have a look at the evolution of packaging, and you will see that we have gone backward since the eighties, as there were talks of implementing sustainability then, which have completely been abandoned since the mindset of scarcity took over. Can you imagine that, in the eighties, Coca-Cola was sold in glass bottles and recollected after usage in a reutilization cycle? This concept was given up because plastic proved cheaper and lighter, and you would not have the hassle of taking back the bottles. So the "price" was "externalized" and passed on to the environments.

It was ultimately the duo of politics and economics that permitted this development to happen.

If we wait to let the market take care of the resulting environmental calamities, you can bet that we are doomed. One can understand the absurdity of such a claim and the fallacy that a "customer" should take care of these problems and the absurdity of "voting with their purse." The idea that we let markets decide what is "cheaper" in a global market, without laws and regulations in place to guarantee that practices can be sustained for longer periods, is pure madness. This is the shortsighted wealth-creation mentality in its essence.

But there are many other common practices in the economy that are done for the sole purpose of maximizing profits - hardwiring wastefulness and discharging the footprint on us all. An example is Amazon, which has established the practice of destroying millions of returned and unsold items. Once they are returned, they go directly into a big grinder and get destroyed. This is done according to "internal policy," for reasons that may have to do with the fact that the cost to return, repackage, and resell opened items might be higher for Amazon than simply destroying them.

Many practices like this are common across all industries, and it is an insider secret that the managerial boards are completely aware of, as these are internal policies of companies and tolerated by governments. It is free-market dogma in action that we should let market players auto-regulate themselves and that "the market will know best." The market players have developed measures to counterbalance the price pressure and artificially raise prices. Many practices, such as this, are done to utilize the concept of wastefulness to induce artificial scarcity of products, which will lower the available goods and decrease supply.

The example of the car industry comes to mind; it selectively involves hiding away cars. There are photos on the internet of tens of thousands of cars standing still in huge parking lots - rusting, unsold. This is all documented, and it is done to raise prices. It is not that nobody would buy them, but if you sell the unsold cars for $500, then who will buy the $20,000 cars? Many products will never be used, and in a lot of cases, they will be thrown away without one day of utilization and will end up in landfills, polluting the environment. Is that good economics? No, it isn't.

This race for lower prices and the complete lack of regulation threatens our economic future and any certainty of an intact environment. Lower prices will inevitably lead to products of increasingly lower quality and safety standards. By putting more pressure on the producers in this way, unsafe food and products will be the result, as well as worse working conditions, horrific conditions in intensive farming, unsafe disposal of dangerous substances, and so forth. We have built these industries on waste. As the concept of sustainability is blacked out in the current ideology, exploitation is the only way to have added profitability.

A further well-kept secret inside the industries is that of the practice of manufacturing products that are not long-lasting, since long-lasting products will delay the next buying cycle. Products are intended only for the short and medium-term so that the next profit can be generated sooner. This is causing manufacturers to have to build cheaper to ensure profits. It is clear to any three-year-old that products with lesser quality will be short-lived due to lack of adequate planning and production.

Another huge problem that is caused by this mindset of scarcity is the heavy use of chemicals that, since the inception of industrialization, have been used heavily and are the epitome of raising productivity to create wealth with long-term sustainability being sacrificed. It is this idea that made them favor chemicals over natural alternatives at the start of industrialization some 300 years ago. And while they had their reasons to have more productivity, with our modern economies of incredible efficiency and demand elasticity, it is ridiculous and incredibly damaging to continue with those malpractices. It is, therefore, of no doubt that the true price of production in such an economic "environment" will be paid by the natural environment.

This is especially the case in poorer regions! Take the clothing industry in Bangladesh and the immense environmental catastrophes that are piling up there as a result of bringing cheap clothing to the first world nations. The rivers are poisoned. The air is poisoned. The ground is being poisoned. This is a common practice of the globalized economy nowadays because the concept of competition creates steadily worse conditions in an unregulated market.

Another example and a huge mess created by this sort of "economy" are the malpractices that are characteristic of the food industry, and the common practices that have been established have now become "tradition." This creates the conditions to maximize production but at the expense of quality and overproduction. To counterbalance these price pressures, the food industry throws away huge quantities of vegetables, fruits, and dairy to lower prices artificially, as the uncontrolled supply and demand determine the worth of their work. Now, I'm not blaming the producers for this; that should be clear. It is bad economics in the first place that does not impose the right measures to resolve this problem at hand, without the solution of imposing new mindless regulations that are often more of a hindrance. It has to be resolved at its source, at an organizational level, in the theory of economics. Regionality, in this case, would surely prove more beneficial.

The heavy use of chemicals in this industry to make it more "profitable" is widespread, as many chemicals are more effective and faster acting than their safer natural alternatives. So, it makes sense to use them if you lack wealth. I will now state a short example. In meat production sites in southeast Asia, the use of *diclofenac,* an antibiotic used to minimize the risk of contagions, is having and has had a tremendous effect on vultures, which have now almost disappeared. This practice is common in intensive farming. It turned out that, because they were eating the carcasses of intensive farming animals, *diclofenac* had a deadly outcome for them. They died as a result of the influence of this particular chemical, and the population has now declined in the past decades by 98%. Therefore, the use of chemicals to maximize profit/productivity doesn't work because we are sacrificing big parts of nature.

Out of their belief in scarcity, it made it more "profitable" to use chemicals as they are apparently "more effective" and faster acting than their safer natural alternatives, so in the belief of "productivity will save us," it makes sense to use them. We could take the example of the extreme exploitation of the earth in intensive farming to illustrate this point - due to the use of fertilizers to maximize yield in the short-term, it renders the grounds unproductive in just a few decades.

The use of medicine in intensive farming and the use of artificial pesticides to maximize the yield of crops and fruits are also harmful. After 100 years of heavy usage of pesticides, we have what scientists call the "insect Armageddon," with huge declines in all species - reaching a 60% decline from 30 years ago. As a consequence, birds have declined too.

We are ripping huge holes in these ecosystems with outdated practices. The misconception is that the "price" will be higher if we do away with these shortcuts, as it would shrink productivity. The truth is that it would not at all be more expensive; the cost would ideally make up further spending, and besides that, there would be just as much of an expansion of economic activity if we focus on sustainability. We would go back to a more natural way of doing agriculture, and there would be only positives, no trade-offs. The expansion of the economy would give more people jobs and therefore result in more spending in the economy. This isn't rocket science, yet we persist with the absurd idea that only productivity can save us from poverty, and while productivity may have some utility, in the current efficient economy/society, the problem need not exist any longer.

Many developing countries have caught up with us and greatly surpassed us in their harmful practices, unfortunately. While some pesticides have been banned in the west, some extremely harmful chemicals are still in use in 3rd world countries, doing immense damage to many species or outright wiping them out. Pesticides are extremely dangerous for wild pollinators, wild bees, and all the related wild pollinators, especially *neonicotinoids*.

With the globalization they have adopted, the extremely wasteful neoliberal system has taken over the worst vices of the wasteful western societies, which have managed to relocate production to developing countries with the result of extreme pollution and destruction of nature on an epic scale. China has had huge economic growth for many years now, and they have turned their country around from a relatively lesser developed nation to a global player with a huge need for resources. They have been the production site of the world for many decades, and they have argued from a financial point of view that it is now their turn to consume.

They may have created financial wealth but at the expense of their environment and ecosystem.

With their huge "progress" in economic growth and rising living standards, they have replaced old cities with new ones. The change they have had in a few decades has never been seen in history; western societies pale in comparison. The damage they have done to their ecosystems is irreparable; they have poisoned every corner of their lands, even much worse than their western counterparts have ever done. Heavy industries have made them dismantle their environment at an even greater speed, in the race for productivity at the expense of ecosystems, much more so than their western counterparts.

The tremendous economic growth combined with the lack of governmental oversight have created a model in which 85% of toxic waste is not treated properly and is disposed of directly into the environment. As there is not enough industry dedicated to the treatment of toxic waste, a black market has created itself to dispose of these toxic substances illegally, which end up dumped in the environment. There is currently not one place in China that is not contaminated with toxic waste.

Toxic waste has been thrown into the oceans and on the land, in many cases creating hazardous zones where whole segments of the population are now at risk of dying and getting sick. There are many cases with images of tons and tons of dead fish washing ashore in China, poisoned by toxic waste in the water. A sign that they may have realized that it will not work out in the long-term is that they were still taking waste from Europe, importing trash to degrade for money, until last year. Maybe the destruction of your environment just for financial wealth, a mere accounting practice, is not a good idea after all. Exporting trash to 3rd world countries - isn't that the most extreme sign of a dysfunctional system?

The sheer scale of destruction in some of the emerging countries due to a lack of regulations, corruption, and lack of control by the authorities is possibly the worst thing that could happen to the outlook of longer-term prosperity for the whole world. When you question the validity of such a system and get accusations such as being anti-prosperity, it is laughable. Well, now we have seen what obsessing about growth and increasing productivity has gotten us into.

The worrisome thing is that 300 years of mass production and a hundred years of fossil fuel and global trade, without sustainability at its core, have caused us to reach extreme boundaries of what nature can take. The system that economists have created has long broken its premise to organize the productive system optimally. In the last 100 years, there has been an exponential increase and speed of the severity of our footprint; productivity at the expense of nature has taken on astronomical dimensions.

But let's continue the argument. We have reached the extreme productive limit too. We have reached the boundaries of nature. The abuse of fossil fuels and chemicals associated with free-market ideology has created artificial growth, meaning that, from this point on, due to climate change and the degradation of ecosystems, productivity can and must be scaled back! The consequences of bad economics have been paid for by the environment, but this will have repercussions on the economy sooner or later, as we will have to deal with shrinking supply. In many cases, this will drive up prices, thus creating bottlenecks that will have a real cost on poorer people. The developing countries are not (yet) realizing that this sort of lifestyle will be very short-lived, as the 21st century will be radically different from the previous centuries; the conditions to guarantee the unsustainable lifestyles are rapidly disappearing under our feet. They came late to the "breakfast" of consumption of the ecosystems but will have to pay the consequences too, as it is a worldwide phenomenon.

I think it can be safely said that sustainable production

methods would not only be of more quality and just as cost-effective but more profitable and sustainable too. Just benefits, no tradeoffs. Changing systems of production like this would be without tradeoffs as the materials, such as plastics for any gizmos, could be easily replaced by natural fibers such as hemp. This is also for clothing or car interior parts, which would not only equal but, in many cases, even be superior with the safer, more sustainable characteristics that we are looking for. Some politicians still go on and claim that we need more production. Well, we need production that is sustainable, and we certainly need new politicians, that's for sure... but what we need are more voters who know economics and vote such politicians out of office. Many argue it is costly to create a green economy, but the message from this book will be that it would create many new jobs if accompanied by the correct economic understanding.

We need to reshape (reorganize) allocative capacity in our systems through laws and regulations for an astronomically better outcome.

II

ECONOMICS FOR THE
FUTURE

6

THE AFFORDABILITY PARADOX

I N THIS SECOND PART, I will propose a change in direction and possible policies and scenarios that bring us to a healthier direction. So, how do we get out of this financial mess of poverty and scarcity I described in the first part of this book? What is the right cure to alleviate the chronic conditions of deprivation while also rendering the system sustainable? It would be very nice to return to the feeling of the 80s when people had a sense of financial security, and the majority of the middle class lived happy lives, with parents that didn't have to worry so much due to the hardships that are so common today. We are having a revival of movies and themes from these years because these were years of worrying less!

What is hindering our society is the phrase that you so often hear these days from politicians, media, and economists alike, which is: "We can't afford it!" It has entered the collective mind by now. It is believed to be an unalterable reality that, despite having the greatest skills, knowledge, and resources in the history of the world, we seem to lack money even to do basic things. I hope I have ripped a door open in this book for you to let you see the absurdities and the mysticism that permeate such a mentality. You will hear about our "debt" problem that we will have to repay, and it is argued that if we spend now, we will burden future generations, and they will have to repay it for us. We even have a counter called the national debt clock, which measures exactly how much we owe the debtors.

So what about the debt?

On this topic, first, we need to dispel and remove the absurdities that have been fed to the public by the lack of knowledge of neoclassical economics and on which the clear insights of MMT excel. The reality of things is that the "public debt" is not an issue at all but a necessary and normal state of things if you want the private sector to thrive. Yes, you heard that right. It is the normal state of being for a healthy economy, and this is due to the nature of what public debt represents for the economy and for the private sector.

Bonds, which are "financial instruments," were used in the era of the gold-standard to raise money for government spending by "loaning" money from the private sector to not endanger the gold reserves-to-money ratio. When they had to raise spending, and the number of gold reserves did not permit an expansion of the money supply, they would emit bonds, which would be repaid in the future with interest and were sold to the private sector. So, it was an instrument used to protect the gold standard when a government required extra funds. There is a great misunderstanding about what debt is and what its purpose is in the modern system. The bond instrument, which private banks generally buy, is, in this day and age, obsolete under a paper money system and not used to raise money "for the government." It is still used out of the convention, and the central bank uses it to do operations of monetary policy

So the bond instrument, which was used as a way to raise spending from the private sector in the gold standard era to protect the gold-to-paper ratio, in the world of paper money, contrary to mainstream belief, is used to set the interest rate by "adjusting" the amount of reserves in the banking system. Bonds will effectively "freeze" reserves out of the banking system and store them away, so the central bank adjusts interest rates with the right quantity in the internal banking system (interbank system), where too many reserves or too little will drive the overnight interest rates up or down respectively. The central bank will buy and sell these financial instruments in what is called the "open market" to target the interest rate, so bonds are a tool (in our day and age!) to assess the **cost of money**, and not strictly for financing government expenditures.

In today's world, bonds are sold as an interest-bearing instrument that is mostly bought by private banks and hedge funds, as well as owned by the central bank itself. An important fact to know is that the central bank provides the funds for the banking system to buy these bonds in the first place, so it is an illusion that we are constrained to our current levels of spending or that we have to rely on the private sector to finance public spending. The thing about bonds is that they will be paid with money that the government has already created, so naturally, the effective buying of these instruments that came after it came into existence.

Public policy foresees that, every time the government spends more than collected taxes, it will emit bonds to "raise" spending. This is a political constraint more than a financial constraint, as it is a relic of past eras. It is prohibited to finance the treasury in a direct, straightforward way. Instead, the central bank does it through the banking system, but the fact remains that it is the central bank that creates money in the first place, so it works directly in parallel. The government does spending by buying goods and services in the private sector using tax revenue plus "deficit spending," which is newly created money through bond-issuance. Running a budget deficit means injecting more money than you take out of the system with taxation. The sum of all the deficit spending by the government is calculated in the "national deficit." This is done to guarantee a working infrastructure and provide social services, such as pensions, welfare programs, and so on.

The fundamental differences between the two methods of money creation

What is of importance is to understand that the two ways of money creation, namely deficit spending and bank loan money injection, have radically different behaviors in the economy. The first way, as we discussed above, is the way of injecting new money into the excess of taxes through deficit spending. The second method of money injection, as we said earlier in the book, is for the banks to give out credits/bank loans to individuals and businesses; in this way, the banking system effectively brings new money into circulation. So, spending, both on the side of the government by deficit spending and through the banking system granting loans to the private sector, forms the basis of injecting new money into the economy. Taxation, on the other side, is the way to extract money out of the economy. This is the regulatory mechanism called "fiscal policy."

Both forms of money injection have significant differences that will have radically different effects on the economy, so it is crucial to understand the differences in money creation through deficit spending versus bank loan money creation. The fallacies about government spending are that, generally, people and classical economists alike don't recognize what government spending does on the accounting part of the economy, compared to bank loan money injection in the marketplace. It has made government spending the only way for the private sector to run a net surplus and have financial wealth accumulation. Let me explain this. The main characteristic of government spending is of vital importance to the economy, as it creates the possibility for the private sector to have a net surplus, in other words, to have actual savings.

The reason for this is that money created by government spending is **_debt-free_**, contrary to the money creation through bank loan money injected into the economy, which will have to be refunded. Bank loans have to be repaid with interest, while money created by the government does not have to be returned. It stays in the economy in cash and mostly in bank accounts and makes up the sum of savings held by the private sector. Yes, I know this might seem confusing, but the reality is that the "national debt" that these idiots want to balance is actually what permits the money to be saved on the part of the private sector to exist. Public debt equals the private surplus, with the profits and savings that the private sector can run in a fiscal year. Do you still want to balance the budget?

This makes government spending the only possibility for the private sector to have a surplus, a cushion of cash to be retained after taxation. The public deficit is, in other words, the private sector's surplus in a double-book entry money system such as ours. It needs the government to take on "debt" in order to run profits and retain financial wealth. With only bank loan money, the tax would bring the private sector progressively further and further into debt. This is exactly what happened since the late 8os with the policies of austerity, and the private sector got further and further into debt because bank loan money can be used to pay taxes in the same way debt-free money does.

To sum it up, deficit spending, or what they call "going into debt" on the part of the government, is a net addition to the private sector without a debt counterpart. It is just an accounting practice after all, like the example seen in the second chapter with the double-entry bookkeeping method, and the offset is private savings - public debt. The "National Debt" is nothing more than the sum of total government spending in the economy accomplished by issuing bonds that does not have to be repaid, which would mean we nullify the private surplus/savings, and it can go on forever as it is the natural state of the economy to have a cushion for the private sector. Media personalities claiming to be experts on the economy will go on TV and declare that we need to "balance the budget" - that it will give more space for the private sector and raise productivity to exit the recessions that their foolish policies of austerity provoked in the first place.

The contrary of deficit spending is running a budget surplus and should be done only in periods when the economy is over-heating or at full speed, as it will tax out more money than it (deficit-)spends, which will also shrink the net-saving chance of the private sector. Generally, to accommodate an expanding economy, countries run budget deficits and, only in a few instances, have a surplus.

The myth of debt monetization and "printing money"

If we mention the idea that we are going to pay for things by using the central bank to create new money to buy "this new debt" you will hear accusations of "running the presses" and that this "debt monetization," which they assume is direct financing of bonds by new money and that it will "debase" the currency and will make us end up like Venezuela, with hyperinflation as the result and money losing all worth and purchasing power.

The reality is that this is all <u>bullshit</u>. It is a story propagated by neoclassical economists out of pure ignorance as to how the modern FIAT money works. It is based on an entirely flawed understanding of the money system, but also how the relationships of the triangle of government-banking system-private sector work in reality. An incredibly stubborn belief to remove these days, believed almost universally and propagated across the whole of society, is the belief of money printing, which is completely fallacious and **does not** represent the realities that we find under the current FIAT money system.

The thing is that the term "money printing" is a completely erroneous one, which comes out of the gold-standard period, where you would have too much paper money in circulation to guarantee its convertibility. In other words, the wealth that you had stored in the vaults at the central bank was not enough to "guarantee" the worth of the money in circulation in the form of paper money. But even that doesn't make sense, since this was more about the difficulty of coming by gold reserves to protect the ratio than actually having too much money in circulation. The origins of these completely fallacious ideas lay in the middle ages when you had the landlords debasing the coins by declaring from one day to the other that they are worthless, or as was commonly believed, they would dilute the quantity of gold in them with other less precious metals, thus decreasing their worth.

The term "money printing" is entirely misguided, since it is again based on the wrong assumption that the government will "dilute" the value of the currency by "printing too much money," associating it to the "debasement" of gold. Since in a paper system, all money is created out of thin air, this is not the way inflation originates. Second, it is impossible to "dilute" the intrinsic value of paper money, since the effective value of the paper is zero, and it doesn't hold intrinsic value as a gold-coin would. The value of paper money is the result of enforced governmental monopoly through taxation and penalties in case of tax evasion.

Since the creation of financial wealth is no problem, what is the limit to spend? In other words, can the government go on and "create" money indefinitely? The answer is no because, as I mentioned before, there are hardwired limits. To return to the topic that we set out at the beginning of the chapter about the idea that, if we can afford it, does that mean that, with paper money, we can spend unlimited amounts in the economy? Technically, yes, but you would break the system. It is essential to understand that the limit of such money creation is not in "inflating the currency" or the "quantity of money," but instead, it is found in the productive system of a nation. It is there and only there that we should look for what is called inflation, namely price increases or "too much money chasing too few goods," which is the textbook definition of inflation.

We find limits in the real production of an economy and its output capacity, as each industry will only produce a certain quantity of goods in a certain amount of time. Therefore, there are tangible limits in the economy, such as labor, natural resources, and efficiency of production (productivity). Again, the limits are not on injecting too much money or "debasing of currency" as the mainstream believes, but rather it is when we are at full employment and a maximum productive speed that we reach the limits before possible inflation arises.

It can increase until we reach the current productive capacity, and the economy will "heat up," and it is at this point that the system has to be slowed down. When the economy is at full speed, ideally, we need to cool it by cutting spending and taxing more. The current situation, though, is that we are running our economies well below their real potential. Our problem is currently one of little inflation, with the economy stagnating due to too little spending. We are running the economy severely under its capacity, so these discourses make little sense for now, also for the simple fact that private indebtedness is at record highs. From here to "screaming" inflation is still a long shot.

Our room for spending in the real economy is not confined to such trivial parameters as debt-to-GDP ratios, which say little about the economy. If the economy reaches full employment, the risk of inflation may increase, and as such, there are hard-set limits to spending into an economy. The current reality, however, is exactly that of too little inflation. Inflation is generally heavily misunderstood, and some moderate inflation on the economy is to be welcomed, since it brings a "forward motion to the economy," rather than the current deflationary forces. Inflation also creates demand and provokes more supply of goods, so it is positive in moderate amounts and its economic effects.

Monopoly issuers of currency can't default on their debt!

We don't run the risk of going bankrupt either, since a monopoly issuer can always come up with new money. That's right; you can always make up new funds in the current system, and you are not constrained by ratios or reserves of the old commodity currencies. Why shouldn't a state that creates its own money not be able to come up with the necessary funds without the risks of going into bankruptcy?

On a federal level, a monopoly issuer of currency such as the US, Great Britain, or Japan cannot technically go into default. As such, as we have stated, they have an unlimited capacity to come up with new funds under the FIAT money system. This does apply only to the federal government and not to the single us-states that behave in such a way as a household or a firm, as they are all currency users. These can very much encounter limits in spending, unlike the central government on a federal level that is the issuer of currency. These same rules don't apply to the Euro-zone that has the European central bank not under its control to work together with its fiscal policy.

The Euro currency, in this sense, has several limitations due to the imposition of budget limits and the European central bank being disconnected from the various central governments of each nation and their fiscal policies; thus, it is like adopting a foreign currency when a country "converts" to the euro. The current crises in Europe have a completely different origin than most think. Most European countries subscribed to fiscal rules that are completely based on neoliberal policies, so they have effectively built their euro-currency on unsound economics. They will sooner, rather than later, have to implement some modifications to the monetary system of the euro because, by now, the richer European nations, such as Germany, can only sustain their balanced budgets by having an export surplus. They will all go into a heavy recession sooner or later, due to very strict limits for budget deficits, and the government heavily underspending will create a lot of private debt. Also, the economy is going further and further in the direction of neoliberalism, with austerity and the complete removal of stabilization by laws and regulations.

In such a system, you run the risk of default, as you are subjected to market pressure in government financing, and you run the risk of bottlenecks in recessions by less taxation coming in and ever greater needs to pay interest on the debt. It is at this moment that market pressure rises and, once financial constraints outstrip the incoming revenue, you are on the path to default. The simplest way to solve this problem is to make sure the European central bank will keep the interest rates low by simply stating that it will guarantee the debt in times of crises, which would take away the pressure, and to overwork the parameters that constrain the governments in ridiculously low percentages of public spending compared to GDPs. So the European problem right now has nothing to do with "socialism" as some conservative circles may put it. Instead, it is like they adopted a foreign currency, as they do not have the power to do what is vulgarly described as "money printing."

We can afford all our aims and goals!

Just look at all the expenses the government is paying out on in the US or elsewhere, and the reality is that this money is not at all a redistribution from tax money, nor is it taken away from the private sector, as is wrongly assumed from the "crowding out" effect. It is simply not a reality under the current FIAT system. The government is in charge of the creation of new money. Hell, it even says it on the banknotes that carry the name of "federal reserve note" and "The United States of America" in the case of the US. Where should the money come from, if not from the government itself? From the Martians that visit the earth once a year!?

As already stated in chapter three, the commonly held belief is that the government has to act as a household, so the notion that it first needs to tax to spend is completely erroneous. It is counter to the realization that money is spent first and taxed later. Such was the example of the newly founded colonies on US soil, where they first put out treasury certificates to operate government expenditures and soon they were accepted in return for the payment of taxes, as the supply of money from the European mainland were scarce, so these certificates would be effectively used as money and doing the same thing as we do today. This is a good representation of the money system that we have, with these certificates being stored in bank accounts as digital numbers of bank reserves or the dollar bills used for the everyday exchange of goods.

Obsessing about balancing the accounts when the issue does not exist under the realities of the current system reminds one of Don Quixote fighting against windmills. In the year 1900, we built beautiful cities, with beautiful streets and sidewalks laid with handcrafted stones. Since then, we have gone several steps backward. We can't afford the most basic things, not to mention addressing the huge environmental challenges that await us. The reality is that a government that has a monopoly on the issuance of FIAT Money can afford almost anything without the fear of inflation or going bankrupt.

7

RECLAIMING THE STATE

THE WHOLE IDEA behind de-potentiating the state is based on the wrong assumption - that laws and regulations are in the way of our economic prosperity and the idea of the perfection of the self-regulating market. To go forward, we will have to reverse most of these disastrous policies and reinstate a government that takes on the role of guaranteeing the fundamental conditions that we want to see in the economy. Contrary to many people's assumptions, laws and regulations would not represent a cost. If one wants to look at the market of job creation, it brings about an expansion of the economy, and it would make the economy "grow." Contrary to the paradigm of the "strictly necessary" economy that we have now due to austerity, we would create the ideal economy that takes care of many of the human needs while, at the same time, guaranteeing the sustainability of the economic machine. Herein lies the secret of the failures of the past 50 years. Regulating industries would not decrease the "wealth" of the private sector in any way, as part of the resources would just be used to address the sustainability side of the economy.

The depotentiation of the government will severely limit the durability of the system, since it favors short-term malpractices over sustainable ways of doing things. Once you understand the fallacies that brought us into this mess, then you will see that the answer is: the economy is perfectly expandable, and by enforcing laws and regulations that target sustainability, we go back to economics that "thinks" with the future in mind. There is some good news: the system isn't broken; it just needs to be taken back and regulated according to what we want.

We don't need to have a complete change of the system; we have to remove the faulty ideas and bring back control of the system, along with the power to regulate it, and set the aims and goals more in line with a sustainable future. We have an incredibly effective tool at our disposal, as we can set the parameters in the economy to reach the aims and goals that society will truly benefit from. The current state creates deprivation for most people, a two-class society with extreme disparity, allowing a minority to possess the whole world. It creates unaccountable monsters in the economy that have the power to compete with governments, and that will run completely on what is profitable, often causing huge environmental problems that favor short-term profits at the expense of long-term sustainability.

Again, the example of the plastics in the ocean comes to mind. What you should do instead is enforce a plastic ban, two years from now, and that in turn will force a market solution. You use the individual entrepreneurship to come up with a solution, confirming once more that regulations do benefit us and actually "create" jobs. The thing is that, if the government doesn't force a resolution of the plastic disaster by enacting a transition period and later an outright ban and forcing heavy regulations on the producers, we will slip into ever greater environmental disasters.

Such economics of scarcity can be rejected without a doubt since it has no future anyway. That will not mean we have to go back to older utopias at all, though you often hear the conservative side raising such specters as communism if government action in the economy is proposed. It also won't mean over-regulating the economy, which is the current state we are in, with laws targeting small businesses and leaving out the big transnationals that create huge monopolies that buy up the smaller competition. There would be no escaping capitalism, but it would signify creating an economy that we want to have and, most importantly, avoiding one that we don't want to have.

Many of the practices that we discussed in the last two chapters in the first part of the book are damaging to our society. It is damaging us with huge social "costs" of unemployment, drug problems, crime, etc. It is damaging the environment. Changing our ways is inevitable, and we don't need to make any tradeoffs to do it.

The role of the government

The government, along with its tools (namely the monetary system, laws, regulations, and the taxation system), can incentivize and disincentivize any behavior it deems destructive or useful for society. This complex societal system we call government is an advanced and comprehensive model of directing society for its purposes and works pretty smoothly.

Only a government can enforce a sustainable economy, and this is true for most things. It works in conjunction with the elected officials that set the direction that we want to go. The maligning of governments has an explicit connotation, and the reality is that governments have been incredibly efficient in their action, contrary to the belief of waste that is generally regarded as true when governments do something. We have to set the agenda, and then a government is actually a pretty efficacious tool. Again, this doesn't mean we should overload the system with unnecessary things from the side of government; the government should accommodate all the reasonable necessities.

I think that guaranteeing the public interest is always preferable to that of a small group of those profiting at the expense of public safety. That's the whole idea behind government, and markets tend to become dysregulated if this principle is not observed. Nobody benefits from poisoned drinking water or pollution in the cities. Whether rich or poor, everybody has common interests that should be placed above all private interests. The government is the tool for enforcing the safety of these interests. To repeat, the way forward is pretty simple: we can afford it without any problems, and we don't have to "punish the customers or the working class." Laws and regulations that go towards a sustainable economy will benefit them, as it is an expansion of the economy that is much needed anyway.

This has no cost at all. It will just redistribute some profits to take care of the whole cycle of a product. It will allocate some resources to guarantee sustainability. That's all. If we intend to enforce a different economic model of taking care of the whole product life, even after the end-of-use, corporations or governments would be the ones taking care of product safety and product afterlife. If we cherish the liberty and safety of the people, we will not support the structures that act out of pure self-interest at the expense of all else. That's what you get when you remove the original protector of the common interests, the government.

The problems of global trade

We can assume the adoption of such a model by the leading nations is going to have a chain reaction on the others. Therefore, this is the way to go. Not only that, but enacting a plan of full sustainability successfully would certainly require us to take back sovereignty or to reform some of the over-structures and transnational organizations that regulate trade, as the process of globalization went on and the governments ceded some sovereignty to them. In this sense, the leading countries have to take on a leading role once more, to have a global outreach, since we face these problems as "one nation of humanity" so to say.

Global trade, by the organizations that promote unregulated global markets, should be reformed in the direction of sustainability by the respective countries, as we have to shape regulations to force healthier economic realities. I think the concept of regional economies has to be implemented, as it is closer and more accountable to the people it serves, and it will be immensely more sustainable. Products, mostly the same in many parts of the world, go from one continent to the other, often causing a huge transportation footprint. There can be an assumption that this would raise prices for the consumer; the reality is that regional economies would grow and accommodate needs locally, which would redistribute the profits locally as well. Accompany it with the removal of austerity policies, and you would create a much more prosperous economy globally by going for regionality.

The whole system could be moved in that direction, and it would only be a matter of regulations and incentives to encourage what we want and disincentivize what we don't. That's, by far, the superior first step to transition our economic system to a sustainable model. Global trade would be much better off by implementing a "distance tax" on products and materials. We would increase prices with a progression of distance, meaning, the further away a product or materials have to be imported, the higher the tax. Important to note here is that worldwide trade would not be banned but disincentivized at the expense of a more regional business, which should be the preferred sort of deal that we wish for. This is no problem from a "wealth" perspective, as prices would just be allocated differently, and higher costs in an economic environment with adequate liquidity would translate into higher wages as well.

So it's not that we would lose out on "wealth"; it would just reorganize most of the economy towards a regional scenario, while still leaving intact the possibility of having trade with more extensive parts of the economy. This will be done while guaranteeing local manufacturers access to the needed resources that cannot be acquired in the regional markets.

Incentivizing a fully green economy

Enabling a green economy would have the proper "side effect" of moving profoundly towards the full occupation, too, so this is politically highly doable, and it would benefit the regular people the most. Once the system is understood and the "too much debt" voices are silenced, we could immediately begin moving towards full occupation while reshaping the economy into a time-proof production system.

This process of transition towards a fully green economy would rely heavily on exploiting the "good greed" by using the law of demand to the advantage of all in society. By creating the demand with laws and regulations and setting out a period to transition towards a green economy, we could force the market to come up with the necessary skills, knowledge, and behavior. The best minds in the private sector would come up with the solutions to implement it, using competition to our advantage.

The use of taxation to incentivize and disincentivize what we want is highly desirable. By using tax to adjust prices to reflect the real cost of the impact of the materials we are using, as what is the actual value of materials that are not compatible with sustainability such as single-use plastics. The real cost of such materials that will stay for many generations in the environment and create hazards for animals and humans alike are astronomical, and their price plus their tax has to take that into account.

Biodegradability should be a primary factor for the use of any materials in the industries and their manufacturing of products. There is an array of materials in nature that are equal and sometimes even superior to chemical ones, besides being astonishingly more sustainable. All that is a perfect reason to remove the mindset of the "free" market religion, so that we can change and shape society with the ideal goals we wish for. We could do it right away. In a decade, we would partially be independent of fossil fuels and could transition immediately to natural alternatives such as hemp bio-fuel.

A "new green deal" is the way to move forward, and it is in agreement with the rising sentiment of these days - to have a positive vision for the future, as half a century of free-market economics has rendered the outlook of most people grim and pessimistic. Such a deal would signify that we are going to start to address some of the incredibly urgent environmental problems and, at the same time, create the conditions for a positive outlook for the people. The voters would accept this as an affirmative political action that would make their lives better in all aspects. One step we will have to make is to change from a "consume and throw away" economy to a system that is more in line with sustainable production and using only available resources.

We should enact the most effective ways to regulate such behavior, be it with incentives, regulations, or bans. Indeed, it would have to be made progressively to leave industry enough time to manage the adaptations. This is how politics has done many such things in the past. The state is an incredibly efficient tool to shape behavior, and that doesn't mean only by enacting a lot more regulations but by having a few rules in place that show the desired results. Right now, we have a lot of regulations that are a burden for the regular people but do nothing to bring advancements of any kind. At the same time, our goal has to be that of a reutilization of things as much as possible with a focus on how to produce items that can be reused.

The afterlife of products in the current situation is, at best, ignored. There are specific industries dedicated to the disposal of the waste of our productive system; still, the common practice is the burning of waste in incinerators, which produces substantial carbon emissions. The best way to address this problem is always at the source. Going biodegradable and removing as much waste as possible from products. Regulations need to ban as much of these practices as possible, and if it is at the expense of the "shininess" of the finished product packaging, then so be it. Hemp plastic is the sustainable natural alternative, or should we say plastic is the environmentally costly alternative to hemp plastics.

Enacting such a model by law would require the knowledge of science to determine the best model to guarantee that products have a sufficient shelf-life and utilization cycle. Governments, in conjunction with the private sector, would come up with a solution that should take each component of a product and make it reusable in some form, finding a way to reutilize metals, plastic, and other materials. The viable solution is a system of reutilization of the already created resources. The government could and should assist this crucial passage in our industries. If there is a lack of private-sector entrepreneurship, we could do this by helping the new markets and, if necessary, creating industries with considerable government spending, and in later periods, selling it at market prices.

By introducing the idea of the "lifecycle" of a product from its inception to the end-of-life of the products, the new industries would have a system to break it off and, in an ideal scenario, even reutilize its parts in their entirety. The question if it would be financially viable, I will repeat one more time, is a resounding **yes**. The cost could be easily "paid" by forcing the companies to pay outright or "create" such industries with laws and regulations, which would incentivize the private sector to invest in such areas. A tax credit would certainly help to incentivize businesses to show that their products can keep for more extended periods, and we would undoubtedly have to mandate a minimum period of integrity for these products. Regulations and an "abundance market" of enough funds would set adequate minimal conditions in the economy, below which things are not safe and/or sustainable. The market would be "up-spiraling" rather than the current down-spiraling movement.

The thing is that products made of quality would have their durability increased; this is a wished-for development as we want to break the cycle of cheaper and lesser quality. We need quality products, made safer and more expensive to guarantee a decent profit to the producers and a fair wage to laborers. Bans should be instituted for materials that are too dangerous. We could effectively set bans to have it completely removed from production. In this sense, a properly funded government can utilize the full potential of the law to prosecute illegal behavior. Furthermore, we should do away with governments spending huge sums on subsidizing ultimately destructive industrial practices and whole parts of the economy, such as intensive farming.

Setting a time to replace the current industries of environmental disasters to fully functioning sustainable ones is vital. Political support is already extremely high in the population for environmental solutions, so there needs to be an awareness of the real possibilities. It is doable in a relatively short time if we wish it. Put the regulations in place and work it in stages, impose the rules, and once the market forces intervention, then the experts will generally come up with the necessary knowledge. What it would take is an abandoning of the wealth-gap mentality and the enforcement of a fully working, funded state that sets rules for sustainability and enforces the transition.

We should gradually enact fiscal policies, for example, rewarding all-natural clothing production and increasing taxation on those who still use older, harmful production methods. This is the way to solve our environmental problems by using the full potential of the money systems in conjunction with a functioning state! These tools, if used properly, are incredibly useful; this is not rocket science. To bring on change, you force it along an accommodating period. The only variable is how to implement the ways of doing it optimally. The regulating power of the state would guarantee better conditions for producers, consumers, and of course, laborers.

Rejecting the "market-perfection" dogma is the first step, as only by reinstating the government and shaping desired outcomes will we address these problems. I think the approach described in this chapter has been somewhat of a common sense approach - the conclusion is that it is in the interest of all to have a functioning government.

8

SHAPING A PROSPEROUS AND SUSTAINABLE SOCIETY

I WILL ARGUE in this chapter that the best way to enforce sustainability is to have prosperous conditions for a middle class in place, as only a prosperous middle class will guarantee all the right conditions in the economy to take care of the full economic cycle. The most efficient way of organizing things is the creation of middle-class society, and getting away from an oligarchy structuring of power would allow greater distribution of wealth in society, as wealth in the hands of more people would make environmental exploitation less necessary.

What we have now is what we could call "oligarchy economics," where austerity drowns all that is strictly necessary for an economy. Therefore, a middle-class society of economic prosperity is also a sustainable one. Currently, we have an economy of maximal competition, which forces laborers to take on every job, at any condition. Austerity puts pressure on businesses as the profit margins and wages get squeezed. This is a cycle that will reinforce itself further and further, as discussed in chapter four. We can decide what kind of society we want in this sense; it is a political decision. It is inevitable to get away from the idea of maximal competition and relax the conditions in the economy by expansive measures on the side of the government.

Our production systems are running heavily under their true potential, causing us to have unemployment. Therefore, we need the balancing force of a debt-free monetary policy, as the indebtedness of the private sector has resulted in this vanishing of the middle class. A good analogy of the productive system can be seen as pictures in our minds of the engine of a car; the more potent the engine (the productive means, productivity), the more fuel we can inject (money injection) and the higher the performance (output of goods and services).

This makes it a mighty engine, and the driver will decide the road we want to take. There is no problem reaching full employment. It is merely accepted ideologies that don't want us to achieve it. We can easily aim at what can be seen as full employment and, at the same time, create the means for a sustainable economy. We have already discussed the idea of inflation in chapter six, and actually, moderate increase is a prerogative of a healthy economy. Conservatives will scream "socialism!" but I hope I have made a good argument that too little government intervention in the economy is hugely damaging. We can see that European societies are more balanced in that sense and have fewer problems, such as widespread poverty and so forth, at least in the northern states where austerity measures have not been implemented. All forms of government today are a mix of two systems, governments assisting the private sector (socialism) and those who allow pure market economy (capitalism).

We could say that herein lies the distinction between what communism and capitalism are, with the difference being that competition and ambition are used in our system to achieve efficiency. Human ambition puts people in the competition, with the winner of this race generally (idealistically) benefiting themselves and society at large. It is a motor of great incentive for people to do their best, which also helps society at large. The problem with this current type of competition is that it has taken on a disparity of gargantuan proportions. We don't need unlimited competition. It has created a society where few individuals own much of the world's resources and hoard away money from the economy, endangering democracy, since these people hold everything. This can't be what we want.

While we certainly want competition, we can choose how much competition we want to have, as few individuals taking on all the financial and physical resources is an awful way to allocate resources. The way to conceive the cornerstone of society that we want is to favor the creation of a prosperous middle class. This should be one of our aims, as this kind of society will take care of itself and its sustainability, as well as guarantee enough resources for all. The economics that we should focus on is one of the favorable outcomes for the working people on low wages, which make up the massive majority in the economy and who will immediately spend the money, thus putting it back into the economy. Planning for favorable conditions will result in raising wages, with money spent back into the economy right away, to a point where we have a surplus of funds besides basic needs, in which case we can start to pay down debt and build up savings. This should be our economic blueprint that will bring back a healthy middle class.

The reality is not so, as most people barely have the funds to sustain themselves. This has to be the base of what I call middle class-economics, namely building the cornerstone of society around the premises I have described above. The way to have a healthy economy is through a very simple logic: raising spending for those at the bottom of society will inevitably lead to a positive economic result, as the evidence suggests that money travels upwards. Generally, those on high incomes don't spend money and put it back into the system but, instead, store it away from the system. It goes into investments and, in the worst cases, into tax havens.

In that sense, contrary to all this mantra of trickle-down, the evidence suggests that markets always function from "bottom-up," meaning the money generally travels from the bottom up to the top. The wealthier classes absorb wealth for the simple reason that wealth "brings" wealth based on how the system is built. Wealthy people will get wealthier on auto-pilot after they reach a certain point of wealth due to the unfair taxation; wealth will be stored away at the top. The right way to go forward, in my opinion, is to have a serious discussion about what kind of society we want and what purpose those billionaires serve. We will have to tackle inequality, as a few hundred people owning half of the world's resources is an inefficient way of operating, not to mention unfair from an ethical point of view.

As we have already disproved the idea that it is only the private sector that creates all the wealth, they will have fewer excuses with their mantra of "job creation." I would say that many of these billionaires are a big strain on our middle classes, since not only do they hoard away huge quantities of money, but all that money doesn't initiate the economic circle from the bottom earners. The other thing mentioned is that their purchasing power will cause price hikes for those with low incomes, too, as they have disproportionate buying power. Further, not only do they put a significant strain in the sense of financial wealth, which we have seen is no problem to create, but on the resources side of the economy, as well as the accumulation of housing of the upper classes that drives up the prices of homes across the world.

It is no wonder that housing is so expensive and is in the hands of a few big cats, while the majority is struggling and don't have proper shelter. Isn't that the negation of the concept of economics and suboptimal allocation of resources if we have many houses remaining empty and, at the same time, affordable housing being almost non-existent? So, where is the solution or, better yet, what is the problem? The problem is in oligarchy politics, as inequality brings us to this huge market disequilibrium, so we have to resolve that first.

While it is certainly an advantageous approach to anchor the living minimum wages through the law, which is no problem from an affordable perspective, as we learned in this book, there should be talks about anchoring a sort of maximum wage, too. The question is this: what good does it do to have people that own billions in resources allocation more than money, who will hoard away that money and make a new business cycle more problematic. They hugely distort market prices and purchasing power. The question is, what good does it serve a person to have more than

500 million in euros or dollars? It doesn't serve any purpose from an organizational point of view since the system guarantees his survival in place, and the competition necessary for private enterprise to guarantee an efficient supply of goods is fully guaranteed to reach a level (an example) of 500 million euros or dollars. This would guarantee a private sector that still relies on competition, such as the one we have now but without the excesses of a few individuals owning half the world. This is just a stupid fetish of some people that are addicted to the hoarding of money.

The other aspect is that they have been favored by laws and regulations that they helped lobby for with enormous repercussions on the environment. This strikes as common sense to me, guaranteeing enough profitability and competition for the private players in the economy, while also having a system in place that can ensure sustainability.

Tax away excessive inequality

This makes taxation an incredibly valuable tool, with which we can design what kind of competition we want. So, do we want competition that results in monopolies and disparity, or do we want to have a minimum and a maximum wage? Well, we would not call it that; we could tax after a certain amount of 101%, which would terminate the pathological obsession and fetish of hoarding money or physical resources. We would help them in a certain way, as they seem like rather unhappy people. Tell this to the Koch brothers, and let's see how they react. Nevertheless, it is the common sense approach, in my opinion.

Taxation is an incredibly powerful stabilizer as well, particularly a progressive taxation system, as is present in all the developed nations. The more you earn, the more you will pay, and that's only fair. However, in the current form, the lower classes pay a much more significant share of their income, and this further exacerbates disparity and should be reversed. A progressive tax is one way to enforce the critical aspect of equality, but it is also a stabilizer against the boom and bust cycles of the economy, as, in crises, shrinking incomes pay less, and in boom cycles, they get in the higher quota, thus balancing out the imperfections. One of the best ways to counterbalance the hoarding of financial resources is proper old redistribution, which will serve to counteract the disparity that is exacerbating the differences in purchasing power.

Redistribution works because it takes away wealth hoarding from the top towards how the economy works: bottom-up. Too big a rift between "rich and poor" makes the system unstable because, on one side, you have rich people hoarding financial wealth and the allocative power, as well as physical resources. This will make it hard to have the right amount of liquidity in the system. An more equal society with the right amount of competition is thus preferable, or you will encounter problems of political and economic instability. Taxation is used to enforce equality, not to raise taxes! This is a considerable insight under a paper money system. We could very well take the taxed money and erase it, and it would not make a difference from a technical point of view in money creation. It is just more in line with the narrative that taxes pay for things, which is the widespread belief and a relic of the pre-paper money era. With taxation, besides enforcing the demand for currency and giving forward movement to the economy - just like the engine of a car that needs gasoline, it serves as the primary stabilizer on various fronts, mainly inflation.

A further stabilizer and a way of guaranteeing enough money tokens remain in the economy and savings for the private sector is a concept known as *"universal basic income"* (UBI), which guarantees the funds that government spending can't reach. This money would otherwise be earned from what could be called unproductive jobs. Not that, economically, it matters too much if you have a productive or unproductive job, but for various reasons, it is better to aim for productive employment. While the government has to use its spending to satisfy the needs of the private sector by investing in schools, infrastructure, and so on, a universal basic income is still a logical necessity. What we have seen until now in this book is that, if you remove the fallacies and the ideologies, what comes to the surface is a potent machine to shape society in the way we want.

This begs the question - what do we want?

Instating a third way of money creation: the Universal Basic Income

We cannot go on like this, with ever-increasing productivity, growth, and the like. People are consuming resources. People are desperate to make a living. It all leaves a considerable carbon footprint. We need to move away from this paradigm of manual work toward a more carbon-neutral society. What is strange is that we have collectively pictured in our minds the image of an ideal society that we aspire to have. We wish for a community that lets people chase their dreams, build on their talents, provide excellent conditions for their families, and so on. We all agree on that, and if you conduct a survey, you will likely get a 100 percent approval rate of these ideas!

And, who can blame them? Is it utopian thinking to desire a world where all people can invest in their talents, instead of continually being bogged down and at risk of financial ruin? I don't think so. A universal basic income would be the second option for debt-free money injection, and a further stabilizer for the economy. It would ensure that there are enough money tokens as well as space for savings for the private sector in the system, which, in the current order, is only possible as a counterbalance with more government spending.

UBI has several plus points concerning government spending:

It takes away the account of it all since this money would go into the bank account of each individual. A basic income is much cleaner in that regard. It injects money from the bottom-up, and it has no particular maintenance "cost" of real resources such as people utilized on the accounting of it all. The basic income would be implemented instead of unemployment money for the low income so that a minimum of funds would be guaranteed to any unemployed person. It acts as an anchor for decent living wages, as the minimum for unemployment would be measured as a living wage. This also acts as a measure of control where a downward spiraling market will not be able to employ people and pay them less and less. It would take away the political dependence that government spending creates. We would have money in the hands of the private individuals, and they would decide what to do with the money - this should be welcomed! This would limit and shrink government action in the economy, which could then only focus on providing the underlying infrastructure to a nation. It would free up a lot of resources needed to administer the whole government spending, such as welfare programs, etc. It is in the best interest of all to go towards this form of debt-free money, instead of relying on government spending to create the proper favorable conditions in the economy.

The thing is also that you would inject debt-free money into the economy and adjust it accordingly. This is much cleaner than finding the "right temperature" with government spending for creating private-sector savings. Now, of course, it should be carefully evaluated to see the right amount to defy the fears of inflation. Note that I wrote of the fears of inflation, rather than actual increase, as it is demonstrated that, in the current economic environment with free-floating currencies in globalized markets, supply hardly encounters such barriers. Taking away allocative power from the billionaires would certainly create much space for such a measure. Inflationary forces apply normally on singular goods that have price increases, such as the case for oil, but we will hardly ever see what they call hyperinflation. The recent cases of hyperinflation of developing countries have been due to their currency being pegged to a reserve currency, such as the dollar.

Automation: a society of more free time

Not only is it from any point better to have workers work less, but it is also healthier; people work better in shorter periods when rested, and productivity goes up. But it goes further; Ford discovered that people would spend money in their free time, but if they are continuously working, they can't spend money. What is relevant is also that we need to get away from mechanical jobs that can be dehumanizing for many people that are not adapted to that kind of unrewarding work. Automation is the answer to that kind of need. The need for creativity is still, for the most part, untapped, as only a minority of people are responsible for the most critical steps forward in human knowledge, art, and so forth.

If you see the immense frustration in the current rat race, we should know that it is the answer to many of our current needs and crises. It is clear that, in an ideal scenario, people should do what their talents are, while currently, the vast majority of people do jobs counter to their abilities due to the necessities of work. This again is just a symptom of the current failed economics that created the artificial society of scarcity we are currently in. Masses of people that could contribute with their talents and creativity are bogged down in what they perceive as pointless jobs, forced by the underlying conditions of a starved economy and their necessity to make ends meet in an environment of underpaid jobs and fearing for their survival.

The further discussion we want to have is that of how much we want people to work. In the last decades, people have over-worked, sometimes having to work multiple jobs to stay afloat, which has brought on many malaises. The idea that automation is or will take away jobs is only partly right, as new posts will be created. This is fundamental to understand: human needs are endless; we don't encounter a limit on human needs. The thing that most people don't see is that, with automation, we can have many more needs satisfied so that we can concentrate on the good things in life. I don't think anyone can argue that people investing in their talents will have drawbacks.

Automation will be instrumental in that we can lower footprints as the rest of the economy would be much more service-based. And so, we should work much less to take care of ourselves and our families. Working hours should be drastically lowered for all these good reasons, and for the environment; we don't want to have people going out daily to "make a living." Let me repeat this: it is unsustainable for the future. Automation is a huge rise in productivity as machines do things faster and more precisely, so this means less of a carbon footprint on the planet, which is a good thing. It also means a huge expansion of productivity, so we could use that spare time for activities that would further satisfy the needs of society.

An interesting topic is that it could very well generate what could be called unproductive jobs. Well, the same can be said for the substantial over-bloated US defense spending where they employ a large part of the population without producing real value besides armaments, which aren't satisfying the basic needs of the nation, such as housing or supply of food. We could say this is a massive dispersal of resources! This would not be the case with a basic income, as people would spend on their needs and create a more accountable economy that satisfies legitimate needs. Again, the expansion of human needs is endless. We should encourage people to offer their best talents to others, and once they have their basic needs satisfied, people quickly come up with something else they want. So, there is no need to worry that "people will have nothing to do."

As said before, the system is starting to render manual work obsolete, so the economy will logically become more of a service-based economy since production will be more and more automatized. Right now, in the current state of the economy, a lot of the work done (for example, the care of older people or mothers taking care of children) is service based. We could redirect these human resources towards what they wish to invest their talents in. We would profit collectively from such an economy. The needs of humanity are expandable at will. Just take, for example, the needs of 100 years ago; they had fewer requirements, mostly consisting of only the necessities. Not only that, but automation, in conjunction with a basic income, would guarantee that many people, as well as businesses, would not collapse. This is just a common sense approach and a much better way of doing things - the current (mal)practices don't belong in this century anymore. We are much better than that today. And it is a much better approach towards many social malaises stemming out of this system of the scarcity of the past eras, with the crime, drug abuse, overworking, you name it. Almost all "societal" problems have a cause in this sort of wrongheaded economics.

The moralizing approach is producing the contrary result. It has been proven with experiments done by providing people in struggling positions with money, with no strings attached. The outcome has been that these people that once were engaging in damaging behaviors, such as alcoholism and prostitution, if given a chance, actually invested their newfound "free" money in bettering themselves, such as by investing in a business or their education, rather than spending this money on destructive behaviors. If given a chance, people will better their conditions. And a basic income is just such a way to leave these malpractices behind, as well as the ignorance and taboos of older eras, and move towards the next generation of society.

Automation is only a problem in the current downward-spiraling markets that lack money tokens in the economy. If we counterbalance this with a basic income to guarantee enough exchangeability until reaching the desired employment to all, it would be an infinitely superior society than that which we have now, and it is the only logical direction. If we are serious about the environmental crises that are starting to hit us, then automation paired with a primary income stabilizer is the best thing that can happen to us. It is an opportunity to lower emissions since people going to work "to make a living" is terrible for the environment, and we certainly don't want that for the future.

If we are serious about moving towards full sustainability, not only will many industries need to employ more people to deal with the whole product lifecycle, thereby rendering these industries fully eco-compatible and sustainable, but the conservation of nature will play a huge role too. We can employ a vast number of people that are no longer needed, due to automation, and relocate them closer to such jobs. Just look at the huge disasters facing the environment. People will have plenty to do.

This is coming, and whether politics, leaders, billionaires, and the common people want it to or not, this is how the evolution of things goes. Productivity has to be seen as a sparse capacity to satisfy other, new needs. It is not a tool to replace financial wealth.

9

PUTTING IT TOGETHER

W E ARE BURIED in a hole under the current economic paradigm, and we continue digging, not realizing that the exit is in the opposite direction and that we have merely to take it. One way to come around is for all parties to realize the huge advantages of a green economy. It should be crystal clear to anyone that this is not a matter of left, right, up, or down in a political sense but that the future of earth should be in the interests of all! Economics will be the key to conquering the environmental crises, and once the leading nations adopt it, all the world will have to follow, as will the politics involved. And there is a high chance that we have to hardwire sustainability in the economy and "save the world," even though that is a rather tall order.

That's the way the neoliberal doctrine and its proponents implemented trickle-down economics, by hardwiring it into our economic thinking, and nobody ever voted on this, besides electing Reagan and Thatcher! These economic ideas would force political parties and everyday people to follow its principles; the economic doctrines were instrumental in forcing all actors in society to adopt the behavior that they idealized and wished for. They forced the conditions in the economy that we see in our everyday lives.

All over the world, people are struggling, and austerity is hurting so many that the belief in neoclassical/neoliberal policies is starting to fade away. People realize that something is severely wrong with the way that we structure our economy. Globalization has put workers in competition with each other, and they lost out significantly, with the working classes feeling abandoned by the main parties. This is a real crisis by the current brand of economics, and this opens up the opportunity to implement a much saner brand of economics.

The monstrosity of some of the ideas that have been hard-wired in the economic system is the leading cause of our societal downfall. The billionaires and the elites have invested considerable sums in maintaining this system... the good news is that their ideas will ultimately fail as they are based on unsound logic. In this sense, politics plays a determining role in reversing the current environmental catastrophes that are piling up are and are no longer possible to ignore. People are well aware of this situation and change will drive us towards a much better direction. It is only a matter of time and the enforcing of some regulations that will bring the economy towards sustainability. It may take five, ten, or fifteen years, but with our incredible capabilities and our production systems, it would be no problem from an organizational point of view.

Refocusing production and switching from short-term profit

chasing to long-term sustainability is a necessity for the coming decades and no longer something we can postpone. It is an inevitability due to the crises we are facing. We certainly want to have a more human-sized economy with local products, as things moving around the whole world for a slightly lower price doesn't make any sense from a carbon footprint point of view. We will have to move towards a more neutral footprint collectively as a society.

This gives us the need to administer resources that are not endless. If resources are not unlimited, we would have to bound the exploitation of natural resources for sustainability. We can take only so much to be sustainable in the long run. We will have to find a way to allocate scarce natural resources for production. Maybe a right way to resolve this issue would be to have producers "buy a quote" from each individual, which would be shared with the typical population, and they would repurchase it for producing things: sort of a tax on the limited natural resources.

If determined resources are scarce, there are some ways to deviate from the problem, one being that people will use other similar things. Economics will have to be the driver of the car and reshape its theories on the idea of sustainability, and thanks to the insights of modern money theory, we know we can fully afford it. We will certainly have some negative growth, as it is unthinkable to go on like this if we don't want to end up in a scenario where financial wealth is of little importance, as ultimately, the whole economy is based on the ecosystems that supply the resources for the economy.

Currently, politics is subsidizing a lot of damaging practices through government tax credits and outright contributions where we could easily take back resources that were used for these unnecessary aims. We will have to divert resources towards what we want, and damaging practices that take away real resources from these should be abandoned. Currently, we are using dangerous chemicals, and when people get sick, they will spend money at a doctor. This all adds up in the statistics of how the GDP is calculated, so the focus is clearly on producing possible things, but not only does it not benefit society, it is a significant strain on the people.

We should refocus the economy on what we aim to progress as a society and not on mere wealth creation, which has many more negatives than positives. Just look at all the military spending that, more than using financial wealth, is using up a considerable quantity of real resources.

We are subsidizing destructive ways of conducting agriculture that is increasingly damaging the earth, so there is a clear need for regionality and finding concepts that can work us out of the current bottleneck that has been created with rising populations and declining environmental conditions. We must hardwire sustainability practices into the economy with strict laws and regulations. What we need is a refocusing of the economy, not more "growth." The growth paradigm so dear to economists and politicians alike has to be terminated. There is no room for more growth. We need to reshape the aims of our economy towards an *"administrative mode"*, and that will take care of most of the problems.

We will undoubtedly have to use the full potential of the industrial machine that we have at our disposal. Not to produce more but to render the economy sustainable, which is in itself an expansion of the economy, so we can also move towards full employment. A win-win situation that should be easy to sell to voters. To tackle the enormous problems of the climate crisis, conservation of the forests, and so on, there will be a need for a vast refocusing and reallocation of resources, which will be the new prerogative of economics. Thus the main priority is to remove the ideological constraints on spending and ignore the inflation hysteria so we can use the full force of the economic motor to address these issues and make the economy a great ally on this quest.

The good news is that some of the basics of MMT have gained mainstream attention, and some influential people in the financial world have already declared that it will be inevitable for these ideas to take place. The concept of debt-free money through reasonable government spending and the UBI on one side, taxation and laws with the idea of enforcing the acting room in the economy with the fair competition will enable the kind of society that we want - a collectively more prosperous society that doesn't need destruction of the environment to grow. The belief that we can't afford it makes it rather funny to see how humanity would manage to live in a world with a great deal of nature missing. In such a world, financial wealth would be worthless.

The idea of sacrificing sustainability is to be rejected. Since it is no problem from an allocative point of view, the only limit is the human capital necessary to run it, and we have plenty of people that are unemployed or underemployed. Realizing that we have to do some radical changes in just decades to go carbon-neutral, we should take into consideration to use the full potential of the money systems that we have at hand. Central banks should emit "green bonds" to fully tackle this mammoth-undertaking. It is no doubt that a planetary effort is needed, and economics is the key to all of this! The aims should be real human issues, such as full employment or taking care of the ecosystems, not obsessing about the public debt, which is a non-problem.

Can you see the absurdity of leaving unemployed people at home doing nothing while there is an extreme need to have a conservation effort in place, which will take many decades to complete? This can only be regarded as a suboptimal organization of disposable resources that could be more effectively re-allocated without endangering the "public finances." It would be a tremendously good idea to lay out an excellent medium-term plan to go neutral on our carbon footprint and protect the ecosystems but, most importantly, by switching to an adaptive way of doing things towards the environment. We will have to think outside the paradigm that brought us here. There is almost no real talk about planning the economy for the next 5, 10, or 50 years, only 3-4 month period/quarters or a year in advance. They may put out plans for such a future, but it is not taken seriously. In the past century, we had visions for the present and the future. This has all been offered on the altar of the markets and is seen as the oracles that we have to follow: the GDP, the stock market, the prices for this or for that.

We went to the moon in the past century; with the current mindset, we would no longer be able to "afford it." Interventionism and the visions and the aims have to be taken back from the dictatorship of the financial parameters.

One of the most important interventions of a government would be to work with scientists and economists to develop a footprint-index to apply to all of the economy as well as all infrastructure. This would give us a clear path towards sustainability and where the biggest culprits lie. It could be done like this: we would have an index number of a score out of 100 for any activity that is present in our economy. Any value over 100 would have to be banned or modified until it goes under 100. Economics together with politics would be instrumental in moving this score towards sustainability in time, with laws and regulations targeting the worst culprits and, gradually, moving towards a neutral score. The societal model described in the last two chapters could be a good direction to move forward, as it is inevitable that we will need to make such changes in the next decades or even years as the symptoms of failed economics are piling up at an always greater pace.

What this book has proposed is that we have now, unlike prior eras, the knowledge, the tools, and means to have the kind of society that would be truly prosperous. We really can build the society we have in mind; we can ingrain our ideas into economics, and this will reflect in the economic reality. We can build an almost perfect society. Not only do we have all the technical knowledge to achieve this, but we can afford it as this roadblock was a gargantuan misconception of the system to begin with. This brings the ball back into the hands of political movements that can pretty much desire what society we want, without droves of "experts" telling them that this is impossible to do from an accounting point of view, which is ridiculous. Certainly, we are nowhere near what we could achieve. We will have to have courage, visions, and out-of-the-box thinking and enter the "we can afford it" paradigm.

Maynard Keynes summed up the mentality of unaffordability in the society of the 18th century, which has seen a big revival in recent times:

"The 19th century carried to extravagant lengths the criterion of what one can call for short "the financial results," as a test of the advisability of any course of action sponsored by private or by collective action. The whole conduct of life was made into a sort of parody of an accountant's nightmare. Instead of using their vastly increased material and technical resources to build a wonderful city, the men of the nineteenth century built slums; and they thought it right and advisable to build slums because slums, on the test of private enterprise, "paid," whereas the wonder city would, they thought, have been an act of foolish extravagance, which would, in the imbecile idiom of the financial fashion, have "mort-gaged the future"--though how the construction to-day of great and glorious works can impoverish the future, no man can see until false analogies from an irrelevant accountancy beset his mind. Even today, I spend my time--half vainly, but also half success-fully--in trying to persuade my countrymen that the nation as a whole will assuredly be richer if unemployed men and machines are used to build much-needed houses than if they are supported in idleness. For the minds of this generation are still so beclouded by bogus calculations that they distrust conclusions which should be obvious, out of a reliance on a system of financial accounting which casts doubt on whether such an operation will "pay." We have to remain poor because it does not "pay" to be rich. We have to live in hovels, not because we cannot build palaces, but because we cannot "afford" them."

This is a rather good explanation of the ideas behind this all, ideas that are still holding us back two centuries later. We desperately need an informed public that has a grasp of economics and how our economic-political systems need to work together for an optimal result.

I hope you liked this book, but more importantly, I hope you question the current ideas and if we really can't afford the best society.

ABOUT THE AUTHOR

Sometimes a person comes along that doesn't have the qualifications, but is nonetheless the right person to tell a story that could change the world.

The author grew up in Val Gardena, a tourist magnet of a valley in the Dolomites, in the Italian quarter - on the Alto Adige region bordering Austria. He is a painter and decorator by profession with a raging interest in politics, economics, and sociology. He enjoys sports year round, with soccer and ice hockey being two of his favorites, but he also enjoys the simple pleasures of life - like going for a walk with his dog.

If you want to contact the author – Email: Author@romansenoner.com